The Jesus Difference

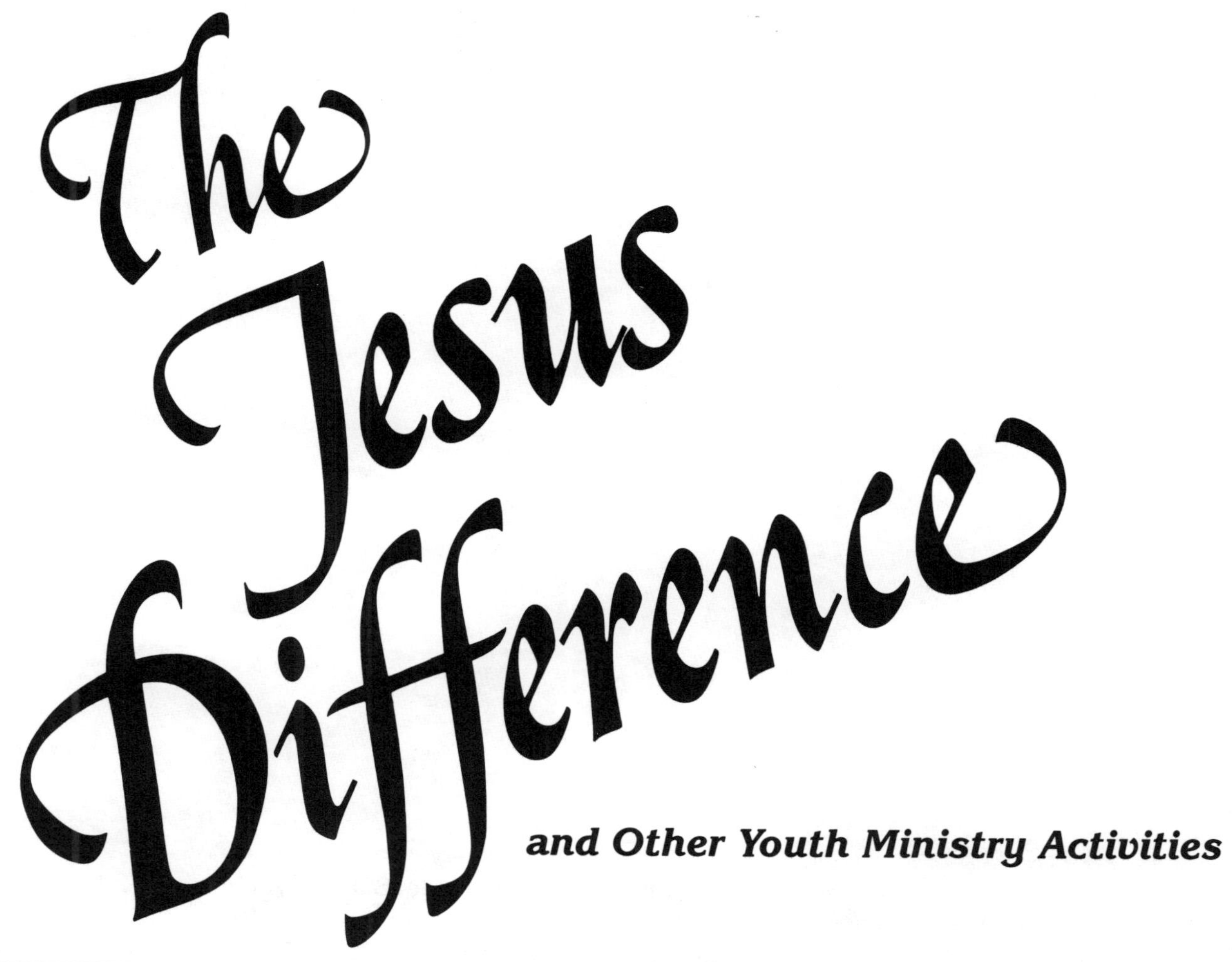

The Jesus Difference

and Other Youth Ministry Activities

KIERAN SAWYER, S.S.N.D.

AVE MARIA PRESS
Notre Dame, Indiana 46556

Permissions

An excerpt from *The Song of the Bird* by Anthony de Mello, S.J. Copyright © 1982 by Anthony de Mello, S.J. Reprinted by permission of Doubleday & Company, Inc.

"Stopping by Woods on a Snowy Evening" from *The Poetry of Robert Frost* edited by Edward Connery Lathem. Copyright 1923, © 1969 by Henry Holt and Company. Copyright 1951 by Robert Frost. Reprinted by permission of Henry Holt and Company, Publishers.

The bible texts used in this publication are from the *Good News Bible*: Copyright © American Bible Society 1976. Used with permission. For the United Kingdom, permission granted by the British and Foreign Bible Society and Collins Publishers, London.

Excerpts from *The New American Bible* Copyright © 1970, Confraternity of Christian Doctrine, Washington, D.C.

© 1987 by Ave Maria Press, Notre Dame, Indiana 46556
All rights reserved.

Library of Congress Catalog Card Number: 86-72571

International Standard Book Number: 0-87793-353-7

Photography: S. Linda Marie Bos, cover, 19, 61, 91; Christina Sekerak, cover; Kathryn Sekerak, cover, 75

Illustrations by Katherine A. Coleman

Printed and bound in the United States of America

Contents

Part Two — Prayer Capsules

Part Three — Communication Capsules

Part Four — Game Capsules

Introduction

The Jesus Difference is based on the total youth ministry* approach to the faith development of adolescents. The book brings you more than 50 "capsules" of youth ministry experiences. An individual capsule is a detailed explanation of how to do a specific youth activity—prayer service, faith sharing process, input talk, meditation exercise, scripture study, values discussion, community building activity or game.

The capsules are like building blocks. They can be used, singly or in combinations, in a wide variety of youth ministry programs: weekend retreats, mini-retreats, days or evenings of reflection, youth rallies, youth-adult evenings, religious instruction classes, and so forth. The capsules in Part One are already combined according to themes. Parts Two through Four contain additional Prayer Capsules, Communication Capsules and Game Capsules.

The activities were developed over the past five years at the TYME OUT Youth Ministry Center in Milwaukee, Wisconsin, by Sister Kieran Sawyer and the staff — Mary Joy Dick, SSND, James Falco, Gerald Fischer, Barbara Linke, SSND, Lucy Nigh, SSND, Dennis Waszak and Gerard Wolf. These TYME CAPSULES are used regularly in the confirmation retreats and other youth experiences offered at the Center.

The activities are intended to be used with groups of senior high youth, grades 10 through 12. While the material has been prepared for Catholic youth, most of the capsules can easily be adapted for use with young people of any religious denomination.

---

*The concept of total youth ministry was developed by the USCC's Advisory Board for Youth Activities in an excellent document entitled "A Vision of Youth Ministry," published in 1976. The vision statement describes youth ministry as "the response of the Christian community to the needs of young people" (p.4). Total youth ministry includes ministry TO youth, WITH youth, BY youth, and FOR youth. Its goals are: 1) to foster the total personal and spiritual growth of each young person, and 2) to draw young people to responsible participation in the life, mission, and work of the faith community.

Vision of Youth Ministry, Catalogue No. P683
U.S. Catholic Conference
1312 Massachusetts Ave., NW
Washington, DC 20005

How to Use the Capsules

The TYME CAPSULES activities are meant to be used creatively. Combine them, select parts from them, adapt them to fit your group and your situation, use them as jumping off points for new ideas. For example, each unit in Part One is a combination of theme-related capsules including small group discussion activities, reflection exercises, meditation time and a prayer service. These activities can be used just as they are presented for a four- or five-hour mini-retreat, or they can become the core of a longer retreat which will also include several other capsules: a morning and night prayer, one-on-one dialogues, love letters, scripture prayer, some fun activities and liturgy. The individual capsules can also be used as single lessons in a religious instruction program. A complete time schedule for a retreat based on "Persons Are Gifts," one of the theme-related units, is found on pages 107-112. This sample plan should give you an idea about how to plan your own weekend retreat.

Adult Involvement

The TYME CAPSULES activities require active adult participation, ideally one adult for every six to eight teen-agers. However, except for the person (or team) who directs the sessions, these adults do not have to put in preparation time. They are present simply as participants, doing whatever the young people do. Their primary purpose is to represent the adult Christian community whose living faith is being shared with the young people. Their presence in the youth activities is essential if the young people are to develop a real sense of belonging in the church.

Several levels of adult involvement are needed:

The Coordinator   This person organizes the youth gathering, chooses the theme or topic, recruits the director(s), sets the date, invites the youth participants, recruits the adult and youth leaders, schedules the place, and arranges for the setting, food, transportation, liturgists, music, and so on.

The Director(s)   This person (or team) studies the sessions selected, prepares the content, gathers the needed materials, presents the input sessions, and facilitates the group activities, prayer experiences and games. It is helpful if the director has teaching experience or has worked with groups of teens in some other capacity.

The Group Leaders   These volunteer adults and youth participate in all of the group activities. They act as small-group leaders and help with the chaperoning of the group. In overnight retreats they are responsible for the supervision of the dormitories. We recommend one adult group leader for every six or seven teen-agers. In an ideal situation every small group has a youth leader as well. Youth leaders should be two or more years older than the retreat group or class.

Others   Involving many members of the total community—parents, relatives, friends, neighbors and parishioners—in the youth sessions helps to develop in the young a sense of belonging in their parish. Members of the parish can be invited to:

- pray for the young people attending the program, retreat, rally
- send *palanca* (letters of spiritual encouragement)
- provide meals or snacks
- provide sleeping space and breakfast for small groups (six to eight) when no retreat center is available
- provide transportation
- help pay program fees
- gather for send-off or welcome-home ceremonies
- attend the closing liturgy

Dialogue: Why and How

The capsules depend for their effectiveness on the interaction of the participants—the interaction of youth with adults, and of youth with youth. This interaction is brought about primarily through dialogue. Some of the dialogue is light, fun and humorous. Its purpose is to break down barriers and to build mutual understanding and enjoyment. It also makes serious dialogue possible. Serious dialogue, the heart of the TYME CAPSULES process, helps the participants to share with one another their dreams and hopes, their questions and doubts, their values and goals, their faith and prayer.

The dialogue process is based on several assumptions:

- that faith is already present in each person, and that dialogue helps to surface, affirm and strengthen that faith
- that each person is a source of truth and wisdom, and that the truth of each individual is meant for and needed by the entire community
- that all people, especially youth, want to open their hearts and share their deepest beliefs and doubts; all they need is listeners who care
- that talking about the deepest values in a person's life helps to clarify and strengthen them for the speaker; a person understands better what he or she has tried to articulate to another
- that the faith of the listener is also strengthened by the dialogue process; one of the most effective ways of alerting a person to the action of God in his or her life is to hear about God's action in the life of another
- that dialogue creates common meanings and values that enable those who participate in it to become a community of faith.

Dialogue of the sort described here can happen only in an atmosphere of openness and trust. To establish such an atmosphere is to a large extent the responsibility of the director. But it is also true that dialogue itself can create such an atmosphere.

Young people learn to share deeply with one another and with adults by doing so. The director's role is to make it easy.

The dialogue activities in *The Jesus Difference* are designed to encourage sharing. Though each activity uses a slightly different dialogue technique, some general methodological principles apply:

Pre-response   Everyone is given a chance to record his or her response in some way before being asked to respond orally. The pre-response might be written, shown with hand signals, or indicated by body positions. The responding is made easy by asking a very specific question with a definite answer, by providing sentence starters, or by giving a spread of answers to choose from. These techniques get everyone involved in thinking about the question, make it clear that there is a spread of opinion on the answer rather than one "right" response, and create the need for an individual to examine a position that is contrary to other positions presented.

Dialogue starters   Getting started with the dialogue is facilitated by designating the first speaker, often in a humorous way; for example, the person with the curliest hair, the person with the next birthday, the person wearing the most faded jeans. Each person then takes a turn around the circle. The starter designation usually creates a little burst of laughter and further relaxes the group.

Pass option   The sharing must always be done freely. If at any time a participant is asked a question he or she doesn't know how to answer, or doesn't want to answer in public, the person simply says "Pass." The pass option is, I believe, the single most effective technique in creating an atmosphere where open dialogue can happen. Given the choice of either answering honestly or passing, young people almost always choose to answer. But the pass option is always there as a safe and easy way out if they are threatened by the question in any way. It is imperative that the pass option be respected by the director and by all the participants.

Gradual deepening   The dialogue moves gradually from light, easy topics to more serious ones. The easier sharing both teaches the technique and warms the participants to one another, thus facilitating the deeper sharing.

Listening   Listening is essential to the dialogue process. Everyone in the dialogue circle shares in the listening role. It is important for all the members of the group to look at the speaker, to respond facially to what is being said, and to ask follow-up questions. The adults should be especially present to each speaker; at the same time, the adults will need to be careful not to become the focus toward which all comments or answers are directed.

Discipline

An important component in any activity with adolescents is discipline. The participants are young adults in many ways and children in many others. Youth leaders vary widely in the kind of conduct they expect from teen-agers and in the disciplinary methods they use with them. I find that the best discipline for youth activities is a well-planned schedule with definite activities that are both enjoyable and involving, and a limited amount of free time.

I also believe in rules—"preventive discipline." I present an explicit code of conduct, explaining the reason behind each rule, and I simply expect the young people I work with to comply. More often than not, they respect this expectation.

A sample copy of the rules we use at TYME OUT, the youth retreat center which I direct, is found on pages 118-119. This may help you in creating a set of rules which fit your circumstances and the leadership style of your team.

The adults who participate in youth activities have a positive influence on the discipline just by being there as co-learners with the young people. They also provide the supervision needed during break times and, for overnight events, are responsible for discipline in the dorms. It is helpful to give the adults a written list of their duties, especially for longer events like retreats. For a sample list, see "Notes to Group Leaders" on pages 120-121. I also recommend giving your group leaders a copy of "Dialogue: Why and How." For your convenience in duplicating, a copy of this material appears in the Tear-Out Section, page 129.

TYME CAPSULES Sessions

The activities found in *The Jesus Difference* can be used in a variety of youth sessions.

Weekend retreats　A two-night overnight is an ideal time span for youth activities. A weekend offers time to provide a concentrated faith experience that incorporates most of the elements of total youth ministry—a deepening of prayer, an increased sense of belonging in the community of faith, interaction with adult Christians and with other youth, and informal celebrations of reconciliation and Eucharist.

One-night retreats　A one-night retreat offers most of the advantages of the weekend. You will often find, however, that it is time to leave just about when the group is getting into the spirit. I do recommend one-night retreats for younger teen-agers.

One-day retreats　I find one-day retreats to be less than ideal, especially if they are held during school hours. The young people seem to have difficulty entering into the retreat spirit in so short a time. However, if you must spend only seven or eight hours with your group, the magic hours from 4 pm to midnight are much better than daytime hours. Rather than schedule a day of reflection on the young people's free day, hold it the afternoon and evening before the free day and let them have their entire day off to sleep.

Mini-retreats and "twilights"　Late afternoon and evening sessions of three to five hours can be very effective for youth activities. I find it difficult to accomplish anything with teen-agers in less than three hours. That length of time is essential if you are to create a sense of community, hold a good discussion, develop an atmosphere for prayer, and have some fun.

Parent-youth evenings　A mini-retreat with a group of young people and their parents can be a powerful communication builder as well as a faith-filled experience for both groups. I usually set up the dialogue groups so that the teen-agers are *not* in the same group with their parents. They seem to be able to relate on an adult level with other parents more easily than with their own.

Scheduling Youth Activities

A facility away from the parish or school is preferred for many youth sessions, especially longer experiences like retreats. Finding a place for a retreat experience can be problematic. It is usually necessary to schedule the facility long in advance, as much as six months or a year. Take care in scheduling religious activities to avoid conflict with important school events like homecoming, prom and major athletic tournaments. Young people should not be forced to choose between the retreat and these other events.

Settings

The capsules use a variety of settings. In an ideal situation the following kinds of spaces would be available. Of course, you will have to adapt to the space you have available.

Large-group presentation space   An area where the entire group can be seated on beanbag chairs, floor cushions or chairs close to the director and the chalkboard.

Discussion tables   A space where the participants can meet in groups of six to eight, preferably around square or round tables. Long narrow cafeteria type tables do *not* work for discussion groups. If small tables are not available, form the discussion groups without tables.

Cozy corners   Comfortable settings where each of the small groups can gather. Couches, beanbags or floor cushions are helpful.

Prayer space   A comfortable area, preferably carpeted, large enough so the group can sit on the floor in a circle. It may be possible to use the church sanctuary for this part of the activities.

"Alone" spots   A space large enough for the participants to spread out for quiet times of individual prayer and reflection (but within the voice and eye range of the director!). The church, gym or cafeteria often can be used for this. A supply of cushions or carpet pieces is helpful.

Pointers on Grouping

The activities can be conducted with any size group provided there is sufficient adult participation, adequate space and a good sound system. An ideal size is 30 to 40 participants, including the adults, broken down into groups of seven or eight. If there are more than 50 in the youth group, it may be desirable to split the group and meet at two different times. One advantage of the split group is that it gives the teen-agers two dates to choose from and so cuts down on absenteeism.

You will need some fast, efficient ways of dividing the participants into dialogue groups. The composition of these groups is important for the success of each session. Each group should contain an even distribution of adult leaders, youth leaders, boys, girls, outspoken and shy individuals, and so on. Try to separate members of friendship groups and *always* separate family members. For most activities it is better not to allow participants to select their own groups.

Some grouping methods are given on pages 116-117.

Handouts and Memory Books

Many of the TYME CAPSULES activities are accompanied by a handout sheet. The handouts are meant to be discussion and reflection guides and should never be used simply as worksheets. Detailed directions on how to use each handout are given in the capsule plans.

The handout masters are designed to fit side by side on a regular sheet of 8 1/2" by 11" paper and folded to form a leaflet. The director can combine the capsules chosen for a particular retreat in any attractive way to form the leaflet. Leaving some pages blank is not a problem; participants appreciate space to jot ideas, reflections and so on. On a longer retreat, the leaflets can be combined into a memory booklet. To make the memory book:

1) Create a cover design to fit the theme of your retreat (see pp. 123-126 for sample covers). Duplicate this cover on slightly heavier-weight paper.

2) Punch a hole in the upper left-hand corner of the cover and of each handout leaflet.

3) Pass out the leaflets one at a time as they are used.

4) Give everyone a 3/4" brad to clip the papers together.

Lap Pads

Procure a set of heavy cardboard pieces about 8" by 10" to use as lap pads whenever there is an activity away from the tables that requires writing.

Music and Slides

Many of the capsules are enhanced by the use of music and video presentations. See pages 113-114 for suggestions about audiovisuals and information on where to find appropriate ones. Some capsules suggest specific music. You may always substitute other appropriate music for that recommended.

Youth Ministry Be-Attitudes

Be Prepared   Study carefully the material presented. Visualize each activity in your mind, "seeing" step by step how it will happen. Be sure you have a clear understanding of the purpose and expected outcome of each. Think through the input sessions, outline them and prepare your own note cards to use in presenting them.

Be Yourself   Use the ideas in *The Jesus Difference* creatively. Make the material your own. Think about it; pray about it; if possible, talk about it with other members of the youth ministry team. Add your own examples, substitute other activities, shorten or lengthen sessions. The program should come across to the participants as yours, not as something you've borrowed from a book.

Be Organized   Have a definite plan of action for the entire program and for each capsule. Be especially clear about directions for the games and activities. Have all the materials you will need ready for quick distribution. (It's best, however, not to pass things out before they are needed.)

Be Flexible   Be ready to adjust your well-organized plan at a moment's notice. Some activities may take longer or shorter than expected; some won't fit the mood of the group; some won't work with a particular group of young people. Always have more material planned than you think you will need. Keep your eye on the clock; if you're running short of time, shorten or drop something—but please, not the prayer capsules!

Be Open   Listen to what the young people have to say and encourage them to listen to one another. Accept their feelings and ideas even if you don't agree with them. At the same time, be ready to challenge them—always respectfully—on positions that are inconsistent, erroneous or unclear.

Be Firm   Maintain an orderly, controlled atmosphere, even during fun times. Do not allow the participants to be disrespectful to you or to one another. Let them know that you expect adult conduct from them. (All of this will be made much easier by the presence of the adult participants in the group.)

Be Happy   Enjoy the young people. Enjoy their nonsense and exuberance as well as their thoughtfulness and serious sharing. Let them know that you like being with them.

Be-lieve   Above all, believe that God is involved in the lives of the young people. Believe that the action of grace precedes, accompanies and follows all of your efforts with them. Believe in the faith and good will of the families and Christian communities from which your young people come. And finally, believe in the youth with whom you are privileged to share the living faith of Christianity.

PART ONE

Theme-Related Capsules

The Jesus Difference

This session helps young people to be more conscious of Jesus in their daily lives. It guides them to ask themselves: Who is this person Jesus? What difference does he make in the world? What difference does he make to me?

A. Preparation

If you use all the capsules in this unit, you will need:

- duplicate handout sheets for each participant. For convenience in duplicating, a copy of each handout sheet appears in the Tear-Out Section, pages 131-133.
- bibles
- pencils
- lap pads
- candles (one for each dialogue group)
- a tape or record of "We Are the Reason" by David Meece (from the album "Are You Ready," Word Inc., Waco, TX), "What a Difference You've Made" by B.J. Thomas (Word Inc., Waco, TX), some background music, and the equipment to play them

B. Grouping

Begin the session with the participants seated on the floor of the large-group area in groups of eight. Later the participants will need spots where they can be alone, and also a small-group area with tables and chairs.

c. Who Is Jesus?
(Stop-Watch Questions)

1. Say:

We're going to share with one another some of our ideas about Jesus. Each person in turn will give a one-sentence answer to the questions I ask. Will the person closest to me in each circle please raise your hand? You will start the answers for the first question. Everyone will add something to the answer till I call "stop." Here is the first question:

When you think of Jesus, what does your mental image of him look like?

2. Allow time for four or five people to answer before saying, "stop." The person who was speaking responds first to the next question:

When you think about Jesus, what do you imagine him doing? Is he preaching? healing? sitting on a cloud? hanging on the cross?

3. Again allow time for four or five answers; then call "stop." Continue in this way using the questions below. Each time you stop, the person speaking begins the answers to the next question.

Which of Jesus' miracles is your favorite?

What is your favorite among the teachings of Jesus? (For example, he taught us that God is a loving Father.)

Do you find anything in the gospel puzzling or hard to believe?

When Jesus was a teen-ager, how do you think he treated Mary and Joseph? (Don't forget the temple incident in Luke 2.)

When Jesus was a teen-ager, how do you think he related to his peers, male and female?

Suppose that God had waited another 2000 years to send his son to earth. And suppose he was born in the USA, in your hometown, and went to your school. Which group do you think he'd hang around with?

When Jesus lived on earth he always paid special attention to the outcasts— prostitutes, lepers, tax collectors, Samaritans. If he were going to your school, to whom would he pay attention?

Now let's imagine that Jesus is an adult in your town. What local problems do you think he'd be concerned about?

If Jesus lived in our world and watched the news each evening, what world problems would he be concerned about?

Discussion:

Pick one of the local problems mentioned in response to the questions and discuss the following as a group:

If Jesus were living now, what would he do about (underage drinking, declining neighborhoods, increased crime . . .)?

4. Allow a longer time for the groups to discuss two or three world problems from Jesus' perspective:

If Jesus were living now, what would he do about (the nuclear arms build-up, increasing acceptance of abortion, world hunger . . .)?

Alternative:

Say:

If Jesus lived today, what would he do about (*give each group a different local or world problem to think about*).

Allow time for discussion; then ask one person from each group to report.

5. End with this question:

If Jesus lived in our world today, how would he die?

D. The Jesus Difference
(Reflection)

1. Give each person a copy of "The Jesus Difference" handout (page 131 in the Tear-Out Section) and a pencil. Then say:

If we are true Christians, the words and actions of Jesus should make a difference in our lives. As followers of Jesus, we should try to model our lives after his, try to base our attitudes and daily choices on his teaching and example.

Read aloud the eight statements under "The Jesus Difference" on the handout, allowing time for the participants to mark their responses.

2. Say:

Now look back over the entire page. As you were doing this exercise, some of the answers probably pleased you, and some of them displeased you. Put a "smiley face" next to one of the responses that made you feel you were living up to Jesus' expectations of you. Put a frowning face next to one area that made you realize you need to try harder to be true to Jesus and his teachings. (*Pause.*)

3. Say:

Take turns around your circle. On the first round, talk about the items you marked with a smile. Talk about the items you marked with a frown on the second round.

E. One Solitary Life
(Prayer Experience)

1. Give each group a lighted candle. Darken the room and wait till all are prayerfully quiet, then say:

I'd like to read for you a meditation I once found on a Christmas card. It's called "One Solitary Life."

> He was born in an obscure village, the child of a peasant woman. He grew up in another village, where he worked in a carpenter shop till he was thirty. Then for three years he was a travelling preacher. He never wrote a book. He never held an office. He never traveled two hundred miles from the place where he was born. He did none of the things one usually associates with greatness.
>
> He was only 33 when the tide of public opinion turned against him. He was turned over to his enemies and went through the mockery of a trial. He was nailed to a cross between two thieves. When he was dead, he was laid in a borrowed grave.
>
> Nineteen centuries have come and gone, and today he is the central figure of the human race and the leader of humanity's progress. All the armies that ever marched, all the navies that ever sailed, all the kings that ever reigned have not affected the life of human persons as much as that One Solitary Life.

2. Say:

How did Jesus make such a tremendous difference in our world? He did it by changing the hearts of people—one heart at a time. He made a difference in the lives of a few simple fishermen from Galilee, and they touched the lives of small communities of persons in Antioch, and Corinth, and Rome. And so the difference spread from heart to heart, from community to community. Jesus can make a difference in my world—my home, my school, my work place—only if he makes a difference in me.

It's that difference that we pray for now. We pray that each of us will invite Jesus into our hearts, into our homes and friendship groups. As we pass the candle slowly around the circle pray silently for each person as he or she holds the candle. Pray that Jesus will make a real difference in the person's daily life.

3. When most groups have finished passing the candle, begin to play softly "What a Difference You've Made."

F. Jesus' Feelings
(Scripture Study*)

1. Distribute bibles and copies of the "Jesus' Feelings" handout (page 132 in the Tear-Out Section). Say:

When I finish giving these directions, I would like you all to move to a spot in

---

* Activity F was created by Mary Joy Dick, SSND, a staff member at the TYME OUT center.

this room where you can be on an "island" alone. Then select any passage on this paper that interests you. Read the passage slowly and try to imagine what Jesus must be feeling in that event. Try to get inside Jesus' skin and feel the situation with him. Then write on your paper a short prayer to Jesus telling him your feelings about that event.

2. When all the participants are settled in their alone spots, play some gentle background music. You may have to walk around the room helping people to find the passages they wish to read.

3. Allow about 30 minutes, then say:

Please return to your groups and share one of the passages you chose. Talk about Jesus' feelings and yours as you reflected on that passage. If you have time, share a second passage.

4. After the sharing time, say:

Please move your chairs back away from the table a bit. (Or: Please move a little more apart.) Put your hands quietly on your lap and close your eyes.

When a quiet presence has settled over the room play some background music to set the mood. Then pray:

Jesus, we thank you for the gift of human feelings. We thank you for becoming human and experiencing these same feelings with us. When we have feelings that are hard to deal with, help us to look to you to see how you would have handled them. We offer to you our fears, our angers, our sadness and our frustrations. We also want to share with you all our joys, our hopefulness, our courage and our love. Help us to be sensitive to the feelings of others just as we want them to be to us. Thank you, again, Jesus, for your humanity and for our own. Amen.

G. **Luke 19**
(Meditation)

1. Meditation is an ancient and revered form of prayer. Every era of the Christian tradition has known men and women from all walks of life for whom meditative prayer was a powerful means of coming close to God and the inner mysteries of human life. Contemporary society has recently rediscovered the power of meditation to heal the human spirit. You may be surprised to find how responsive young people are to meditation experiences like this one.

Explain to the participants that they will be moving to "alone" spots for the next meditation experience. If the room is carpeted, invite them to lie on their backs on the floor. If not, tell them to sit on the floor or on a straightback chair. To meditate well, the spine should be kept very straight, the body relaxed but alert. They should take with them the "Luke 19" handout (page 133 in the Tear-Out Section), a pencil and a lap pad.

2. Say:

Stretch your legs out straight and rest your hands comfortably on the floor beside you. (Or: Put your feet flat on the floor and rest your hands comfortably on your lap.) Now tense all the muscles in your body. Hold the tension for a moment, then relax. Close your eyes. Breathe in deeply through your nostrils, count to four, then blow your breath out through your mouth with a slight whooshing sound. Let's do that together five times. In-2-3-4. Out-2-3-4.

Now keep your entire body as quiet as possible, and your mind and heart as alert as possible as you take an imaginary walk with me:

3. Present a meditation based on the following:

Script:

It's a beautiful spring (or fall or winter) day, and you are walking home from school alone. You're busy mulling over all that has happened in school today—the kids you talked to, the fun you had at lunch, maybe the trouble you were in. You're so deep in thought that you hardly hear your name being called. The person calls again gently. You turn around and coming toward you is a tall stranger. You're not at all afraid, and you wonder why not after all the warnings you've heard about strangers. But when you look again, you realize that this man isn't really a stranger. You don't know how you know, but you are sure that the man walking you home from school is Jesus.

He puts his arm around your shoulder and gives you a little squeeze, and says "Hi, Bill" (or *Patti, or Mary Jo*). What do you say in response? Imagine the conversation you and Jesus would have as you walk along toward home. He starts it off by asking you how school went today. Talk to him in your imagination about your classes, your friends, your school problems. (*Allow two or three minutes of silence. During this time carry on an imaginary conversation with Jesus in your own mind.*)

You're standing in front of your house now. You don't know just what to do with Jesus, so you invite him to come in. You open the door, wondering what your mom will say when she sees the stranger you brought home. You say, "Hi, Mom," and are about to explain about Jesus, but he puts his finger on his lips and winks. And then you realize that your mom doesn't see him. He's only visible to you. Think of the way you usually act when you get home from school. Would you treat your family any differently if you were conscious that Jesus was watching and listening? Take time now to talk to Jesus about your family. Mention by name each member of the family and tell Jesus about your relationship with each one. (*Pause for reflection.*)

You invite Jesus into your room. He comes in and looks all around. How do you feel about your space with Jesus in it? Talk to him about your personal treasures—the pictures on the wall, the things in your dresser and on the shelves, your favorite albums, the award you won in fourth grade. Is there anything in your room you'd rather Jesus didn't see? Since you know he can see everything anyway, talk to him about the parts of your life that you might be embarrassed by or ashamed of as well as those parts that you are pleased with and proud of. *(Pause for reflection.)*

Jesus is sitting on your bed now, leafing through your school yearbook. Talk to him about your friends. In your imagination, introduce them to him one by one. Tell him what you find special about each one, and what you think each one needs from Jesus. If you have a special girlfriend or boyfriend, be sure to talk to Jesus about that relationship. If you don't have a special someone in your life right now, tell Jesus honestly how you feel about that. Is it a problem for you? Take time now to talk to Jesus about each of your friends. *(Pause for reflection.)*

Jesus stands, and you can tell that he is getting ready to leave. He puts his hand on your shoulder and looks at you tenderly. "You are very special to me," he says. Feel his hand on your shoulder. See his eyes smiling at you. Hear him say these words to you: "You are very special to me, Bill" *(Patti, Mary Jo).* *(Pause.)* Tell him how you liked spending this time with him. *(Pause.)* He asks you if you'll spend time like this with him everyday. Can you promise him you will? Set a definite time and place. *(Pause.)*

You walk Jesus to the door and watch him as he walks briskly down the sidewalk. He turns back at the corner and waves. Keep watching him till he's too far away to see. Then open your eyes and sit up quietly.

4. Read aloud the story of Zacchaeus, Luke 19:1-7, and the introduction at the top of the "Luke 19" handout. Ask the participants to work the exercise, using just words or phrases.

5. Say:

Return to your dialogue groups. Take one round to tell your table how the meditation experience went for you. Could you imagine Jesus in your home? Could you really "hear" him talking to you? Did anything distract you? Did you just fall asleep? In a second round, share one thing from your reflection sheet that you are willing to talk about with your group.

Emmaus — They Recognized Jesus

This session can be used with large gatherings of teen-agers, for example, a youth rally or an all-school assembly. With smaller groups, you will probably omit Activities C and J.

A. Preparation

If you use all the capsules in this unit, you will need:

- a microphone, preferably a traveling microphone, especially necessary for a large group

- two people to prepare the dramatization of the Emmaus story

- a tape or record of "Today Is the Day" by David Meece (from the album *Are You Ready?*, Word, Inc., Waco, TX) and the equipment to play it

- eight to 10 volunteer panelists to participate in Activity G (Select teen-agers who are articulate and who represent a good cross-section of the gathering.)

- student facilitators for Activity H (one leader for every eight participants)

- adult moderators for Activity I (homeroom moderators with groups of 25-30 participants work well). Explain the activity to the moderators beforehand.

- duplicate instruction sheets for the moderators. For convenience in duplicating, a copy of the directions appears in the Tear-Out Section, page 136.

- class officers who have been prepared to conduct Activity J. They should also plan and lead the closing prayer.

- duplicate handout sheets for each participant. For convenience in duplicating, a copy of each handout sheet appears in the Tear-Out Section, pages 134-137.

B. Grouping

Begin the session with all the participants seated together in an auditorium or other large area with a raised platform or stage, especially if the group is large. For Activity H the group will break into discussion groups of eight participants. Activity I requires classrooms or other rooms for groups of 25-30. Finally, if using Activity J, a separate large-group area for each class is needed.

c. Stand If . . .

(Getting-to-Know-You Exercise)

Say:

Before I begin today, I need to know a bit about this group. I'll ask you some questions; you answer by standing at the appropriate time.

- Stand if you're a senior.
    Remain standing if you think you might still be a senior next year.

- Stand if you're a sophomore.
    Remain standing if you think freshmen are cute.

- Stand if you're a freshman.
    Remain standing if you think the seniors are wonderful.

- Stand if you think the juniors are the best class in the school.
    Remain standing if the rest of the school agrees with you.

- Stand if you think teachers give too much homework.
    Remain standing if you do it all.

- Stand if you've ever been on a blind date.
    Remain standing if it developed into a real relationship.

- Stand if you've ever been skinny dipping.
    Remain standing if it was daylight.

- Stand if you have a paying job.
    Remain standing if you put money in the bank each week.

- Stand if you've been grounded in the last month.
    Remain standing if you deserved it.

- Stand if you willingly apologize when you're wrong.
    Stand if you're never wrong.

- Stand if you have a little brother or sister who acts like a brat sometimes.
    Remain standing if you love the little stinker anyway.

- Stand if the friendship groups in your school are "cliquey."
    Remain standing if your group is a clique.

- Stand if you have ever felt left out and alone.
    Remain standing if you go out of your way to welcome outsiders into your group.

- Stand if you think you've had enough exercise for this morning.
    Remain standing if you already ran 10 miles today.

D. **The Emmaus Story** (Luke 24:13-35)
(Dramatization*)

Present a solemn reading or a dramatic presentation of the Emmaus story. A simple yet profound way of presenting the story is to have two people in white-face mime the parts of the two disciples as the story is read aloud. Jesus is represented only by their movements and facial expressions.

E. **Scenarios**
(Buzz Session)

Give everyone a copy of the "Scenarios" handout sheet (page 134 in the Tear-Out Section). Say:

The person sitting right next to you will be your partner for this activity. I'm going to tell you several stories. Each one fits a list of characters on your paper. As you're listening to each scenario, decide which character you most identify with or most sympathize with. Circle that person's name. After each story I will give you a few minutes to discuss the problem in the story with your partner.

Prom Date: Tammy is the only one of her group who hasn't been asked to prom. She's been waiting all week for Matt to call, ever since Sunday when Matt's two best friends asked her two best friends, Amy and Lisa. The phone rings, and Tammy dashes to get it. But it's not Matt; it's Kurt. Kurt works with Tammy. He's shy and studious and not very popular, but she likes talking to him. Amy and Lisa think he's a nerd. Kurt hems and haws nervously, and finally asks Tammy to go to the prom with him. *(Remind the participants to circle the name of the character they most identify with and then discuss the story with their partner.)*

Diamond Earrings: There is an uproar at the Berg family breakfast table. Mr. Berg is on the phone with the Colemans, the family where his daughter Kelly babysat last night. An expensive pair of diamond earrings is missing from Mrs. Coleman's dresser. Mr. Berg is furious. He's just shouting something about no daughter of his is going to be accused of stealing anything when Mrs. Berg comes out of Kelly's room with the earrings in her hand. Kelly bursts into tears. Her twin brother Mark starts making lame excuses for his sister. *(Pause for marking papers and discussion.)*

Home Sweet Home: Bob is apprehensive all the way home from school. At lunch he was telling his friends about his new VCR and the videos he got with it, and before he knew it he had invited everyone to come over after school to watch. He knows his best buddy Joe will understand about his

---

*This opening mime and the follow-up activities (H,I,J) were planned by Susan Clark, SSND, and her students, St. Joseph Academy, Green Bay, Wisconsin.

mom, but he's not sure what the other guys will think. He opens the door cautiously and, sure enough, the house is a mess and empty bottles and glasses are strewn all over the place. His mother staggers up from the couch and says, "Hiya, honey, didja bring some friends home?" *(Pause for marking papers and discussion.)*

Party Patti: Three friends are huddled together in the bathroom over Patti's half-slouched form, trying to get her to her feet. Val is really worried. This is the tenth time this month Patti has been so drunk she couldn't stand up. Val thinks they should go for the adult chaperones. Tracy is mad at Patti. It isn't even fun to go to parties with her anymore. But she is sure getting an adult in on things will just cause more problems for Patti. Kristin takes another drink of her beer and giggles. She's a little buzzed herself, and thinks it's all very funny. *(Pause for marking papers and discussion.)*

Report Card Day: Mr. McMullen sits at the table opening the report cards that just came in the mail. Tim has his usual straight-As with an additional note commending him for being accepted into the honor society. Dennis has gone down in everything except art. Geometry has slipped from B+ to D-, and he has an F in biology. Michelle, who puts in hours at her homework every night, has her usual Cs and Ds. Mr. McMullen studies the cards thoughtfully. It's so easy for Tim. Michelle tries so hard. And Dennis has so much fun! He asks himself, "What is the fairest way for me to deal with these children of mine?" *(Pause for marking papers and discussion.)*

All in the Family: There are three teen-agers in the Swanson family. Gretchen has a terrible temper. Ask her to do the simplest thing and if she's in a bad mood, she flies into a rage. Larry is just a grump. He'll usually help if you ask him, but he'll mope all through the job. Tom is easy-going and cheerful and really doesn't mind putzing around in the kitchen. Who will Mrs. Swanson ask to help her with dinner dishes tonight, and tomorrow night, and the night after that? *(Pause for marking papers and discussion.)*

Football Season: Coach Connely has been at West for years. He's respected throughout the conference as a no-nonsense coach who holds to the rules, expects a lot from his teams, and yet who really cares about each young man who plays for him. Good as his teams are, though, he's never won the conference title. But this is his year. Mike is the best quarterback he's ever worked with, Dave is a superb running back, and the rest of the team is strong. School spirit is mounting with each win, and the whole town is excited about the prospect of taking the conference. In a small city like Westfield the success or failure of the high school football team seems to affect everyone in town. The Monday before the season's biggest game Coach Connely gets a panic phone call from the principal. Mike, Dave, and most of the senior players were busted at a beer party over the weekend. *(Pause for marking papers and discussion.)*

Caught: Jodi is a good student and a sensitive caring person. Kim is a hardworking slow thinker who needs all the help she can get just to squeeze out a low C average. Jodi spends a lot of time helping her friend Kim with her homework. But last night she just didn't feel like reviewing for the history test with her. Now Jodi sits at her desk in first hour history laboring over what has turned out to be one of Mr. Kreb's heavier exams and worrying about Kim who will be taking the test third hour. There are lots of answers Kim isn't going to know and Jodi feels she is somehow responsible. She writes out a quick crib sheet to slip to her friend at class break. During the third hour exam Mr. Kreb catches Kim with the answers and recognizes Jodi's writing. His policy is to give an automatic F in the course to anyone caught cheating on his exams. *(Pause for marking papers and discussion.)*

After the discussion time for the last scenario, ask everyone to stand and stretch. Announce a five-minute break.

F. On Learning How to See
(Script)

After the break, present a talk based on the following:

Script:

We began this session with the story of the two disciples who walked with Jesus all the way to Emmaus and didn't recognize him. Don't you wonder how that could have happened? How could they have spent several hours with a friend and not known who he was? The Emmaus story is the gospel's way of teaching us that life after the resurrection is different than life before death. Jesus was alive that Easter day, but he was alive with a new kind of life. The disciples, like all of us who have come after them, had to learn new ways to recognize him.

Imagine, if you can, being a disciple that week Jesus died. Here is this wonderful person you've known for the past three years. You've walked with him from one end of Palestine to the other. You've eaten with him around a campfire and in people's homes. You've fished with him. You've seen him cure a blind man and bring a little girl back to life. You've been amazed and puzzled and frightened and challenged by this extraordinary man. But mostly you've come to love him more than any person you've ever known.

And suddenly he's dead. Not just dead, but disgraced. He has been arrested by the authorities and executed as a criminal. You stumble through the minutes and hours, numbed with the grief of it all. Then you hear a rumor that his tomb is empty! The women say they have seen him, talked to him! You can't believe any of it. You saw the corpse yourself; he was certainly dead. You won't believe unless you see him for yourself, unless you actually touch his living body with your own two hands.

Now let's look at the same problem from Jesus' perspective. He has to convince his friends that he is alive, that it is not just a ghost they are seeing and talking to. But he is alive in a new way. How can he convince them that from now on he will have a different kind of presence in their world, a presence that will no longer depend on the body they have been used to seeing around Galilee? He has to teach them to see in a whole new way. "I will be with you always," he tells them. "Watch for me in every stranger you meet on the road, in every hurting child, every drunken housewife, every lonely teen. You've got to learn to recognize me in all these ways or you won't know that I am alive and still with you."

There's a story I want to read to you which might make the point more clearly. It is called "The Little Fish," and it comes from a book of fables that was originally published in India.

> "Excuse me," said one ocean fish to another. "You are older and more experienced than I, and will probably be able to help me. Tell me: where can I find this thing they call the Ocean? I've been searching for it everywhere to no avail."
>
> "The Ocean," said the older fish, "is what you are swimming in now."
>
> "Oh this? But this is only water. What I'm searching for is the Ocean," said the young fish, feeling quite disappointed as he swam away to search elsewhere.*

Like the little fish, we need to learn to recognize a presence that fills our entire world, the presence of the risen Jesus. We have to learn that Easter is not just an event that happened once many years ago and is over. Easter is always today. The risen Jesus is present in our world today, just waiting to be recognized and loved.

Let's listen now as David Meece sings "Today Is the Day." *(Play the tape or record.)*

G. The Hurting Jesus, the Helping Jesus
(Reflection and Response)

1. Say:

Take your handout sheets again and look at the scenarios. Can you find Jesus in each story? Mark a little cross next to each character who might be suffering. Mark a little heart next to any character who could be helpful in the situation.

2. Invite the panelists you selected for this activity to the front of the room. They will need their handout sheets. Tell the panel:

I am going to be dialoguing with you about the scenarios on your paper. Look at them now and pick one or two that you have strong feelings about

---

*Excerpted from *The Song of the Bird* by Anthony deMello, SJ, Loyola University Press, 1983. Originally published by GUJARAT SAHITYA PRAKASH. Anand, India.

and would be willing to discuss with me. (*Pause.*) Who wants to be first?

Ask each panelist questions like the following:

Which scene do you want to talk about?
Who did you most identify with in that scene?
Can you recognize the helping or hurting Jesus there? Where?
What do you think should be done in cases like the one in the story?
What would you probably do in such a situation?

Conclude by inviting comments on that scenario from the other panelists. Then pick another panelist and repeat the questions with a second scenario. Continue until all the scenarios have been covered.

H. Reflecting and Sharing
(Small-group Discussion—about 45 minutes)

Gather in discussion groups of about eight people (including a student leader). Ask the leader to give everyone a copy of the "Reflecting and Sharing" handout (page 135 of the Tear-Out Section) and then read the directions on the sheet with the group. The student leader will also facilitate the discussion.

I. The Landing of the Ishites
(Discussion)

This activity takes place in homerooms or other rooms capable of accommodating 25-30 people. It should be conducted by the homeroom moderator. Directions for the moderators are on page 136 of the Tear-Out Section.

J. Recognizing Jesus
(Class Forum)

For this activity gather all the seniors in one large room, all the juniors in another, etc. The session should be conducted by the class officers, who give out copies of the "Recognizing Jesus in Our Class" handouts (page 137 of the Tear-Out Section) and proceed with the directions given there. The closing prayer should be planned and conducted by the class officers also.

Persons Are Gifts

The purpose of these capsules is to deepen the participants' sense of personal worth. The activities emphasize that all life is a gift from God, and that all persons are to be valued for themselves, not mere surface appearances. One section focuses on discovering the special gift in handicapped persons.

A. Preparation

If you use all the capsules in this unit, you will need:

- duplicate handout sheets for each participant. For convenience in duplicating, a copy of each handout sheet appears in the Tear-Out Section, pages 138-140.

- a cover for each participant to use in creating a "Memory Book" for the handouts. Be sure the cover features gift boxes in which the retreatants can sign their names during the Closing Prayer (see Activity J., No. 5). A sample cover is shown on page 125.

- brads for clipping the Memory Books together

- a box for every retreatant (boxes can be of various sizes)

- lots of plain white or light-colored wrapping paper (not tissue paper)

- lots of old decorative ribbons and bows

- large gift tags (about 3″ x 5″) like the sample below—one for each retreatant

- scissors and tape

- a set of colored markers for each small group

- pencils
- lap pads
- the videocassette "The Heart Has Its Reasons," a documentary about Jean Vanier and his work with the mentally handicapped. Journey Communications, P.O. Box 131, Mt. Vernon, VA 22121. (optional)
- two adult volunteers to read the poem "Persons Are Gifts"
- a record or tape of "Here I Am, Lord" by Dan Schutte, SJ (from the album *Lord of Light*, NALR) and the equipment to play it

Note: If you have a handicapped person in the program, discuss Activity H with that person before using it with the larger group. The person may even be willing to discuss his or her handicap with you in front of the group.

B. Grouping

Have all the participants gather in a large informal group in a comfortable setting. Plan to move the group to small dialogue circles later.

c. Persons Are Gifts
(Poem)

1. Say:

One of the things we need to learn as we grow into Christian adulthood is how to appreciate people for what they are. Each person in the world is unique and beautiful and special. That holds for me, and for you. But most of us don't always realize that we are special, or that other people are. We don't really look at people; we don't pay attention to their specialness. And we are afraid to let people get to know us because we're afraid they might not like us if they did. It's as if we were all walking around in boxes, hiding our identities inside the wrapping paper.

2. Pass out the "Persons Are Gifts" handouts (page 138 of the Tear-Out Section), pencils and lap pads. Say:

On your paper is a poem called "Persons Are Gifts." Listen as it is read aloud.

Two leaders read the poem, alternating sections. After the reading, ask the participants to read the poem again silently and to underline the sections that are especially meaningful to them. (*Allow time.*)

3. Ask the group members to share their underlined sections with a person sitting near them. (*Allow time for sharing.*)

D. The Outside Wrapping vs. the Inside Gift

(Reflection and Sharing)

1. Pass out copies of "The Wrapping and the Gift" (page 139 of the Tear-Out Section). Say:

> Look at the two lists that describe the wrapping and the gift. In the first list, check the phrases that you feel describe the outside you. In the second, check the phrases that describe the way you are inside.

2. Allow time for checking the lists, then say:

> Share with a friend the phrases you checked and explain what you meant by them. Ask your friend if he or she thinks the phrases you chose to describe yourself are accurate.

Alternative: Read each phrase aloud and ask the participants to raise their hands when you say the phrases they have checked. Call on individuals with their hands raised to explain what the checked phrases mean to them.

E. How Tightly Wrapped Are You?

(Open Discussion)

1. Say:

> Look at the 1 to 10 scale on the handout. The poem says, "Some persons come very loosely wrapped, others very tightly." How tightly wrapped are you? Are you a private person who usually hides your true thoughts and feelings inside? Or are you a wide-open person who lets everyone know how you think and feel? Be careful here. Don't confuse openness with loudness. Some people talk and laugh a lot but use their loudness as a cover. And some people who are quiet in the way they speak and act are quite open about how they think and feel. Mark the "wrapping scale" to show how easily you let people get to know the real you.

2. Allow time to mark the scale, then say:

> I would like to talk to someone who is high on the openness scale — someone who would find it easy to talk to me in front of the group about your thoughts and feelings.

> Pick a volunteer and ask questions like these:

> What are the advantages of being so open?

> What are the disadvantages?

Have you always been this way?

Do you think people usually listen when you are expressing your opinion?

Do you listen when others talk?

Is your best friend more or less open than you?

How do you react when you are with a very private person?

How open are you with:

> your parents?
>
> your brothers and sisters?
>
> teachers?
>
> same-sex friends?
>
> opposite-sex friends?
>
> adults?

3. Say:

Now I'd like to talk to someone who laughs and talks a lot, but who is very private when it comes to sharing "inside" thoughts and feelings. Is there anyone here like that?

If someone volunteers, ask questions similar to those above. If no one volunteers, say:

Does anyone have a friend like that? Can you get your friend to stop being loud and think seriously? How do you manage to get past the external talk to discover the real person?

4. Say:

Is there anyone on the private end of the scale who would be willing to share with us? *(Call on a volunteer or two and ask questions like those above.)*

F. The Gifts You Have and Are
(Small-group Discussion)

1. Move from the large group to dialogue groups of seven or eight people. Say:

Now turn to the decorations around the "Persons Are Gifts" poem on your handout. In the upper right-hand corner you will find a row of gift boxes. Write in each box the name or initials of a person who is a gift to you — not a person who gives gifts to you. Write the big gifts in the larger boxes, and the small gifts in the smaller boxes. You may add more boxes if you need them.

2. Allow time to mark the boxes, then say:

Now we ask each person to tell your small group about one of the persons you put in the boxes, and to explain how that person is a gift in your life. Take turns around the circle, each tell about one person on the first round, one on the second round, and so on, until I call time. The first speaker will be the person who has been gifted with the most brothers and sisters.

3. Make sure each group has completed at least one round of sharing, then say:

Now look at the lower left-hand corner, at the package with the word "talents" written above the bow. Talents are special gifts God gives to each person he creates. Each of us has a unique set of talents. No one has exactly the same talents as mine or as yours. Write one of your talents in each of the four sections of the box. It isn't being proud to say what your talents are, as long as you realize that God, not you, gets the credit for them. And it wouldn't be fair to God to say you don't have any.

Some of your talents might be: art, music, dancing, athletics, bodily coordination, a sense of humor, acting, fixing things, writing, mechanical skills, speed, listening, sensitivity, patience, versatility, good taste, singing, brain power, caring for children, organizing, sewing. *(Read the list slowly, adding others as you think of them, explaining some, naming your own, etc.)*

4. Say:

Now share with your group the things you wrote in the talent box. Start with the person who complained the most about not having any talents.

5. Say:

Another box on the page is the WISH box. All of us wish we had been given gifts and talents we don't have. I have always wished I could be more talented in *(name your own wish)*. Write your wished-for gifts in this box.

6. Allow time for the writing, then say:

Share your wishes and tell your group why you wish you had each talent that you mention. Is it a gift you could acquire if you worked at it? Start with the person who has the longest name.

G. Gift-Wrapping Session
(Optional)

Have everyone choose a box and wrap it beautifully with the wrapping paper provided. This can be done at any time prior to the closing prayer. It is also possible to do the closing prayer with a handout sheet rather than the actual gift boxes (use page 140 of the Tear-Out Section).

H. The Wrapping Is Not the Gift
(Open Sharing)

1. Gather in a comfortable setting for discussion.

2. *Optional:* If it is available, show the video "The Heart Has Its Reasons," a documentary on Jean Vanier and his work with the mentally handicapped. The discussion that follows does not need the video background, but is greatly helped by it.

3. Pass out copies of "The Wrapping Is Not the Gift" (page 139 of the Tear-Out Section). Read the introductory paragraph aloud. Then say:

How well do you know persons who are handicapped in any of the ways listed here? Some of you may have a handicapped person in your immediate family or among your relations. Some may have good friends who are handicapped. Some may just know passing acquaintances. Check the appropriate box for each.

4. Allow time to check the list, then say:

Most of us don't know how to react when we meet a person in a "different" wrapping. Little children sometimes laugh and make fun of the person; adults sometimes ignore the handicapped or are overly solicitous. In the spaces at the right, tell how you respond to persons with each handicap. Use the list of reactions below the chart to help you.

5. Allow time to complete the chart, then say:

I'd like to talk to someone who has a handicapped person for a friend. *(Call on several volunteers and ask questions like these):*

Tell us about the person.

What special needs does he or she have?

What special gifts?

How did you get to be friends?

Was it hard or easy for you to get to know the inside person?

What things can and can't you do with your friend?

What does your friendship mean to you? to the other person?

Have you ever had to defend your friend against people who were mean or thoughtless?

Does your friend ever talk with you about how it feels to have the handicap?

What have you learned by having this special person in your life?

6. Say:

> Now I'd like to talk to someone who has a handicapped person in the imme-diate family or among relations. *(Choose volunteers and ask questions like these):*
>
> What special needs does the person have?
>
> What special gifts?
>
> How has the handicap affected your entire family?
>
> Can you remember learning from your parents how to be caring and understanding with the person?
>
> Has the handicap ever made you feel embarrassed? proud?
>
> Have you ever thought what it would be like if you had that special need?
>
> What have you learned by having this special person in your family?

7. If there is still time left, have the group discuss how each group of handi-capped persons is usually treated.

I. With Love From . . .
(Affirmation Exercise)

An affirmation exercise like this one is a must activity for the closing hours of a retreat. It gives the young people (and the group leaders!) a much needed opportunity to give and receive positive affirmation. Allow plenty of time since the exercise could run from 30 minutes to an hour.

1. Say:

> One of the things we have tried to do during this retreat is to become more aware of the specialness of each person here. We've begun to see that each person is a gift to all of us, and that, once we start paying attention to more than the outside wrappings, we can discover the beautiful inside person each person is and is becoming.
>
> The next activity is a chance for you to focus even more on the special gifted-ness of each person in your small group. This is how it goes. When you get to your small group, take one of these gift tags, put your name on it, and tie it to the box you wrapped earlier. *(Instruct the participants to tape it to the hand-out sheet, page 140, if you did not do Activity G.)* Then decide on one person to be first, probably someone who isn't shy, like Renee *(name an out-going person in your group).* Everyone spend a few moments thinking about Renee and the unique combination of talents, ideals, personality, abilities, and character traits that make her the special and wonderful young woman

she is. Then everyone tell Renee about how you think she is a gift to you and to the world. Try to talk *to* her, not about her. Say something like "What's really special about you, Renee, is. . . . "

After speaking to Renee, each person writes a word or two on Renee's box that sums up his or her comments. When everyone has affirmed Renee and written on her box, she responds by telling the group the kind of gift she is trying to become for everyone. Then she picks the next person to be affirmed.

2. Move to the small groups. *(Have the participants bring their wrapped boxes. Be sure the group leaders take a tag for each person and a set of markers.)* Ask the groups to stay together until everyone has completed the exercise.

J. **Closing Prayer**
(to be used at the end of the retreat)

1. Set up the prayer space. If you made gift boxes, arrange them attractively on a table or altar. You will need two lighted candles (in glass containers) for passing. Ask the participants to bring their handouts when they gather for the prayer.

2. Gather in an informal circle around the altar. Speak briefly, basing your comments on the following script.

Script:

We have spent the past two days growing in our realization of the gift of life. Each of you has been a very special gift to me this weekend. Your cooperation, your enthusiasm, your prayerfulness, your silliness have made this retreat a very gifted time for me.

I have also noticed how beautifully you have been gifts to one another this weekend. Through your caring listening and your open sharing, you have helped your companion retreatants realize that they really are gifts — gifts from God, gifts to the world.

We need to keep alive this attitude of seeing ourselves and others as gifts. Turn back to the "Persons Are Gifts" handout and find the large gift box in the center section. Think now about some definite ways you can be a gift to the people you share life with — your family, your friends, your school community, your parish. Write your ideas in the gift box. *(Allow time.)*

4. Give the lighted candles to people sitting at either side of the room. Say:

Look back over the things you have written and pick one that seems to be really important to you that you would be willing to share with all of us. You'll by saying something like "I want to be a gift to my parents by making the effort to show them that I appreciate all they've done for me" or "I plan to share my gifts of music with the parish by starting a youth choir." We'll pass the two candles around the room. (*Name the person on one side*) will share first, then (*name the person on the other side*) will share. After each person speaks, he or she will pass the candle to the next person. If you don't want to say anything when you get the candle, just pass it on.

5. When the candles have been returned to the altar, say:

You will want to remember in a special way all of these gift-people you have spent the weekend with. I'm going to play the song "Here I Am, Lord." As the song is playing, pass your Memory Books around the room. When you receive each book, sign your name in one of the gift packages on the cover. Let your signature be a prayer for each person and a promise that you will continue to be a gift for him or her. Do this exercise prayerfully.

6. When all the books have been passed, ask each person to pick up his or her gift package from the altar and stand in a circle around the altar. Sing together the chorus from "Here I Am, Lord." Thank the group once more and dismiss them.

Promises

This material can be used very effectively with seniors to help them realize the importance of promises and commitments in building a successful and rewarding future.

A. Preparation

Note: The "Promises" song plays an important role in this set of capsules. Learn to sing it yourself and/or teach it to a small group of participants. (You could ask a few good singers to come early just to learn the song.) Have the group singing the round as the participants arrive, teaching it informally and getting more and more people to join in.

For this session you will need:

- duplicate handout sheets for each participant. For convenience in duplicating, a copy of each handout sheet appears in the Tear-Out Section, pages 141-143.
- pencils
- a large sheet of poster paper or newsprint for each dialogue circle
- a felt-tip marker for each dialogue circle
- small slips of paper for "hat"
- a box (or a hat) to collect the papers
- one candle for each dialogue circle (select candles that cast enough light to read by)
- a bible marked at Genesis 9:8-17
- a recording of "Rainbow" by Darryl Ducote (from the album *Beginning Today* by the Dameans, Teleketics Recording) and the equipment to play it
- a volunteer to do the bible reading for the Prayer Experience. Have the volunteer go over the reading ahead of time, perhaps during the break.

B. Grouping

Begin by asking the participants to gather in one corner of the room, sitting quite close together in an informal cluster. For the Prayer Experience you will need an area large enough for each participant to have space to be "alone." Later in the session you will need a small-group area as well.

c. **If, If, If**
(Opening Activity)

Begin the session with the following series of statements:

If you have your own savings account, raise your right hand.

If there's anything in it, raise both hands.

If you'd like to try hang-gliding, flap your wings.

If you talk on the phone at least five hours a week, hold your right ear in your hand.

If you're a friendly, outgoing person, shake hands with three people near you.

If you're shy, cover your face with your hands (keep it covered for the next "if").

If you're not at all shy, kiss someone whose face is covered.

If you can lift 50 pounds easily, flex your muscles.

If you can lift 150 pounds, pick up the person next to you.

If you told a lie this week, slap your mouth.

If you've got smelly feet, hold your nose.

If in the past week you said the words "I'm sorry" and meant them, raise your left hand.

If you said the words "I love you," cross your heart with your hands.

If you said the words "It was my fault," point a thumb at your chest.

If you usually pray before you go to bed, fold your hands.

If you play a musical instrument, pretend you're playing it.

If you're the baby of your family, suck your thumb.

If you think we've had enough of these personal revelations, stand up.

d. **On Making Promises**
(Script)

1. Give out the "Promises" song (page 141 of the Tear-Out Section). Ask the song leaders to sing it, then have everyone sing in unison until the group is comfortable with the song. Finally, sing it as a round with one song leader bringing in each of the three sections.

2. Pass out copies of the "Promises to Keep" handout (page 141 of the Tear-Out Section). Read aloud the Robert Frost poem (prepare it so you can read it well). Then sing the round once more.

3. Give a short talk based on the following script. Prepare the talk well so you can give it in your own words using your own examples.

Script:

So much in life depends on making and keeping promises. Promises are at the root of our relationships; they are often the basis of our trust in other people. Some promises are spoken—like marriage vows or an oath of office. Some are written—like a work contract or an insurance policy. Some promises are implied—the unspoken promise of constant love and care parents make to their newborn baby, or the unspoken promise to be there for practice that automatically goes with signing up for a team. We expect people to live up to the promises they make. We respect people who keep their promises, and we are rightfully disappointed and even angry with people whose words can't be depended on.

Let's take a moment now to reflect on and pray about some of the promises that touch our lives. Think of the promises, spoken and implied, that have been made to you, and the promises you have made to others. Ask God to deepen all the relationships in your life that are based on spoken and unspoken promises (*read the following list slowly allowing a bit of reflection time after each item*): the relationship with your mom . . . your dad . . . each brother and sister . . . each of your friends . . . that special boyfriend or girlfriend . . . your teammates . . . your school community . . . your teachers . . . your city . . . your country . . . and most of all, your relationship with God himself.

4. Allow for a few minutes of silence, then begin singing "Promises" softly. Sing it once or twice through as a round.

E. Promise Keeper
(Small-group Activity)

1. Divide the participants into small groups. Say:

Let's show the people in our dialogue circles how often we make certain promises. Raise your hand to answer the following questions. How high you raise your hand tells how often you make that kind of promise. (*Read aloud the questions in Section A of the "Promises" handout, page 142 of the Tear-Out Section, allowing time for the hand-raising after each.*)

2. Pass out pencils and copies of the "Promises" handout and say:

Now let's see what kind of promise *keepers* we are. Go back over the questions you just answered—they are in Section A of the handout—and decide how well you usually *keep* each of the promises listed. Use a 1-5 scale (with 1 being low and 5 being high). When you have finished, study the picture of you your ratings present. Based on that picture, check one of the phrases in Section B. *(Allow time.)*

3. Say:

Now pick one of the promises you'd be willing to talk about to your dialogue circle. Take turns around the circle with each person talking about one kind of promise—how often you make it, how well you keep it, how you feel about yourself as a promise keeper, and so on. If you finish, go around a second and third time as you have time. The first speaker will be the person wearing the most faded blue jeans. *(Allow time.)*

4. Give each circle a large sheet of poster paper or newsprint and a felt-tip marker and say:

Think for a moment of how important promises are to civilization. As a group, make a list of all of the aspects of life that require people to be true to their word. In each item you list, explain what role promises and commitments play. *(Allow time. Then post the completed lists and compare them.)*

F. **Personal Commitments**
(Reflection)

1. Say:

A commitment is a deep inner promise made either to yourself or to someone else. In the light of the importance of promises and commitments to our becoming real persons, let's do some thinking about the promises that shape our lives. Ask yourself these questions: Who or what really matters to me? Who or what am I willing to spend my time, my care, my energy, my money on? What am I committed to—what persons, groups, goals, ideals, or causes?

Move back from your circle a bit and spend some quiet time thinking about your personal commitments. As you think, fill in Section C on the "Promises" handout with names, initials, or key words. *(Allow time.)*

2. For the next activity you will need the names of all the participants in a "hat." Give out small pieces of paper and ask everyone to write his or her first and last name. Collect the names. Announce a break, and ask the group to gather after the break in a large group with their handout sheets and pencils.

G. **On the Spot**
(Open Dialogue)

1. Gather again in a large group. Remind the participants to bring their handouts and pencils. Take up the "hat" full of names and say:

I will draw a name from this hat. The person whose name is picked is "on the spot." I will ask that person some questions about the commitments he or she was thinking about in the last activity. We do have a pass rule. If you are asked a question you don't want to answer, you simply say "Pass." If you choose to respond, however, your answer should be as honest as possible.

2. Draw a name and ask two or three questions. Then draw another name, and so forth. Here are some sample questions:

Would you tell us about a relationship that you are committed to? *(You might substitute "team" or "ideal" for "relationship.")*

How long have you been involved in this commitment?

How does the commitment affect your life?

How firm is the commitment?

How much time, energy and money do you spend on it?

What kinds of things might weaken the commitment?

Is it possible that it might die out completely?

How public is your commitment?

How much does your commitment affect other people?

3. Close this section by singing "Promises."

H. **God's Promises and Mine**
(Meditation and Prayer Experience)

1. Say:

Faith and religion also depend on promises and commitments. The scriptures tell us many times that God's relationship with his people is based on a covenant, a promise. The covenant with God is a two-way promise. God says to us, "I will be your God and you will be my people." God promises he will be a loving, protecting, providing God. And, in return, he wants us to be a caring, obedient, loving people.

Faith, then, is an interchange of promises. God promises us his love, and we promise him our love. We know for sure that we can rely on God to be true to his promise. Can he be as sure of us?

Growing in faith means two things: growing in our belief in God's half of the covenant, and growing in our commitment to our half. As our faith grows, we come to a deeper realization that we can always count on God to be true to us. We learn to rely on his love, to depend on him to care for us and for our loved ones. At the same time, growth in faith means deepening our commitment to God, growing in our willingness to make promises to God and to live up to them. We become persons God can depend on to help create a loving, caring world based on his plan for creation.

2. Pass out copies of "God's Promises to Me" (page 143 of the Tear-Out Section) and say:

On this sheet you will find several passages from the Bible. Some of the passages are the words of God speaking a promise to his people. Some remind us of how faithful God is in keeping his promises. We are going to spend some quiet time now meditating on God's promises and what they say to our hearts. Find a quiet spot where you can be "alone," and read the passages slowly, one at a time. Try to hear God speaking the words directly to you. Tune in to what God is saying in your heart through the words of scripture. Don't necessarily try to finish all the passages. You might spend the whole prayer time with just two or three. *(Allow 20 to 30 minutes.)*

3. Say:

Star the one passage that names the promise you most need to hear from God today. Then write your responding promise to God in the space provided. *(Allow time.)*

4. Ask the participants to gather again in their small groups. Give each circle a lighted candle, then darken the room. Say:

One of the earliest accounts of a promise made by God to his people is found in the book of Genesis. After the great flood, God made a covenant with Noah and his descendants, and as a sign of his promise, he set a rainbow in the heavens. The rainbow is to be forever a sign of promise—a sign that after the storm comes sunshine. Let's listen as *(volunteer)* reads for us this ancient promise. *(The volunteer reads Genesis 9:8-17. Toward the end of the reading, begin to play softly the song "Rainbow.")*

5. After the song say:

We ask you now to share with your circle the scripture passage you starred— the promise you most need to hear from God today. Read the passage aloud, and tell your group why those words of God caught your heart.

6. Close the prayer time by singing "Promises" one more time.

Trust Walk

The trust walk is a powerful dynamic for group interaction. It needs to be carefully explained and monitored, however.

A. Preparation

For this session you will need:

- a blindfold for each participant (except the group leaders)
- several copies of the directions for guides. For convenience in duplicating, a copy of this handout sheet appears in the Tear-Out Section, page 144.
- group leaders, one for every six or seven participants
- several playground balls
- several jump ropes
- a copy of the "Trust" and "Hymn of Praise" handout sheets for each participant. For convenience in duplicating, a copy of each handout sheet appears in the Tear-Out Section, pages 145-146.
- pencils
- three bibles (mark one at Mt 9:27-30, the second at Mk 8:22-25, the third at Lk 18:35-43)
- three volunteer readers for the prayer experience
- a record or tape of "He's the Hand on My Shoulder" by B. J. Thomas (from the album *The Best of B. J. Thomas*, Word, Inc., Waco, TX) and the equipment to play it

B. Grouping

The Trust Walk is usually an outdoor activity. An area that provides lots of sensory experiences is ideal—plants, birds, trees, gravel, concrete, water, background activities, even traffic noises in the distance. However, even the most familiar places come alive in this activity.

You will also need a large-group area for the reflection. This could be indoors or outdoors.

Finally, the prayer experience should be held in a semi-darkened chapel or prayer room. This could be a closing night prayer on the day of the Trust Walk. You will need enough light for the readers.

c. The Trust Walk

(Activity)

1. Gather the group, preferably outdoors, and say:

> Help each other put on these blindfolds. Fasten them securely because the exercise won't be effective if you can see even a little. When you are blindfolded, sit down and wait for further directions. *(Everyone gets a blindfold except the group leaders.)*

2. Continue your explanation of the activity:

> I would like you to sit here silently, imagining what it must be like to be blind. In your mind go through just one day and think how that day would be if you couldn't see at all: *(read the following slowly, pausing between phrases)* waking in the morning, taking a shower, selecting your clothes, fixing your hair, putting on makeup, preparing breakfast, going to school, recognizing your friends, attending classes, participating in your favorite sports, listening to music, doing homework, going to parties, going to bed. Since you can't see, try to experience your other senses more keenly. What can you hear? How do things feel and smell and taste?
>
> Soon someone will come, take you by the hand, and lead you on a sensory journey. Go with your guide and do whatever he or she guides you to do. You will have to trust that your guide cares about you and will not let you get hurt. The walk will be done in *perfect silence*, so you will have to rely totally on your guide and your own senses of hearing, touch, smell and taste. Wait now, as patiently as you can, for someone to come to you. It is important that everyone keep perfect silence throughout this activity.

3. Give each leader a copy of the "Directions for Guides" (page 144 in the Tear-Out Section). Ask the leaders to read the directions, then select one blindfolded person to lead on a sensory journey. Continue until all the "blind" have been taken on a walk.

D. Reflection and Dialogue

1. Give everyone a copy of the "Trust" handout. Ask the participants to spend some quiet time thinking about the meaning of the trust walk experience and answering the questions.

2. Gather in a large group to share the reflections.

E. **The Blind See**

(Prayer Experience)

1. Gather in a chapel or prayer room. Say:

Close your eyes and sit quietly for a few moments. Imagine again that you are blind. Try to put yourself back into the time of Jesus and think what it would have been like to have him cure you of your blindness. Keep your eyes closed while you listen to these scriptural accounts of Jesus curing blind people.

2. Readings: Matthew 9:27-30; Mark 8:22-25; Luke 18:35-43. *(Allow some quiet time after each reading.)*

3. Say:

Keep your eyes closed. Hear Jesus saying now in your heart, "What do you want me to do for you?" Answer him. What do you need from him? Maybe you have a blindness that needs healing, a blindness that keeps you from believing and trusting in God, from seeing your own goodness, from finding a way out of a problem you're entangled in. *(Pause.)*

In the reading from Mark the blind man was brought to Jesus by his friends. Maybe you, too, have friends or family members who need Jesus to touch them. Maybe people you love are blinded by anger, jealousy, selfishness, alcohol or some other problem. Bring them to Jesus. Ask him to touch the blind spot in their lives and heal them. *(Pause.)*

The leaders and I will now walk among you, touching each of you with the healing touch of Jesus. When you have been touched, quietly open your eyes. *(Walk among the group, prayerfully touching each person on the shoulder for a few moments. As you do this, play "He's the Hand on My Shoulder.")*

4. After the song, say:

In each of the scriptural stories, those who had been healed praised God for the new gift of sight. Let us now praise him together. The words of Psalm 100 are on your handout sheet.

Value Systems

This activity always engenders an excellent large-group discussion. It helps the participants look closely at some of their personal values—to see where they came from, how they are influenced by family and friends, and what it costs to live according to them.

A. Preparation

For this session you will need:

- lap pads
- pencils
- a "Friendship Frame" handout and a "Value Indicators" handout for each participant. For convenience in duplicating, a copy of each handout sheet appears in the Tear-Out Section, pages 147-148.
- a small, blank card for each participant

B. Grouping

Begin the session in a large, informal group, sitting on the floor if possible. The whole session can be conducted in the large group, or you can break into small groups for discussion later during the session.

C. Friendship Frame
(Activity)

Pass out copies of the "Friendship Frame" handout (page 147 in the Tear-Out Section) and say:

Look at the exercise labelled "Friendship Frame." In a minute I'll ask you to put the initials of your friends in the frame. Where you put the initials shows where that friend fits in your friendship group. Closest to the word *me*, put the initials of the people who usually hang around with you. You may add initials for other clusters of friends—from work, from the band, from the crew of the school play, from summer camp.

Fill in your friendship frame now. *(Allow a few minutes for filling in the friendship frame.)*

D. Value Indicators
(Reflection)

1. Pass out copies of "Value Indicators" (page 148 in the Tear-Out Section) and say:

> Now look at these value indicators. This list of activities indicates the values held by an individual or a group. How is each item viewed by the people whose names you just put in the friendship frame? Use the number code at the right to show whether the item is "in" or "out" in your group. Mark your answers in the first column. You may want to consult with your friends as you work down the list. *(Allow time.)*

2. When everyone has finished marking the list, say:

> Now let's share some of our ratings. I'll call an item and you show by raising your fingers how you think your friends would rate that item. Where does your group stand on No. 1, obeying rules? *(Pause.)* On No. 7, selling drugs to children? *(Pause.)* On No. 24, "BS"ing teachers? *(Pause.)* Are there any other items you would like to see the group's ratings on? *(Call for the ratings on a few items suggested by the group. Do not discuss the issues at this time.)*

3. Say:

> Now we are going to go through the list a second time rating each item according to the value system you were *taught* — by your parents, your religion teachers, your school. Put the rating in the second column. If you weren't taught anything about a particular item, just leave that line blank. *(Allow time.)*

4. After the group is finished, say:

> Now compare the two lists. In how many items is there a difference between the values you have been taught and the values your friends hold? When you have your total, just say it aloud. *(Pause for responses.)*

When all have finished counting say:

> Raise your hand if you had a difference in more than 35 items . . . 30 to 35 . . . 25 to 30 . . . less than 25.

E. How We Learn Values
(Script)

> Let's look more deeply at the question, How do we learn values? Our values come from various sources. Some values are *taught*. Your parents, your religious leaders and your teachers have been trying to get you to learn and live

by a definite set of values since you were very little. You know those values very well—no one had any trouble filling in the second column on the chart—but if you're like the rest of us you probably don't live by them all the time.

Other values are *caught* from the people we spend our time with, especially our families and our friends. Catching values is a natural phenomenon. It isn't bad or good, it just is. Because we are social beings, we adapt to the ideas, attitudes, actions and values of the people around us. We catch both positive and negative values from others. If the people around us are kind and friendly, we tend to be kind and friendly. If everyone is crabby and negative, we can easily be the same. If cheating on tests, picking on unpopular kids and cutting down teachers are acceptable actions in our friendship group, it's easy for us to do those things. On the other hand, we can also get caught up in such positive actions as planning a surprise party for a teacher, working on a benefit walk, or gathering food for the poor.

When this phenomenon of catching values is mostly negative, it's called peer pressure. When it is positive, we are likely to call it good example. In either case, it is a natural part of life for everyone, adults as well as teen-agers. But that doesn't mean we don't have any control over the values we catch from our peers. We need to learn to look critically at the values of the people around us and to make definite choices about which values we want to accept and imitate and which we want to reject.

That brings us to a third source of values, those that we choose for ourselves. We will call those our *thought* values. We can't go through life just doing unthinkingly whatever we have been taught. Nor should we act unthinkingly on the values we have caught from our peers. We need to think about the values in both of those categories, to weigh them against our own experience and understanding, and to choose for ourselves the values which will direct our lives. If we don't make thought-filled choices about life, someone else, either our families or our friends, will be doing our thinking for us. *(Pause for a few moments before asking the participants to turn again to their handout sheets.)*

Say:

Now let's fill in the last column on the "Value Indicators" chart. Go through the list again and think: Where do I stand on this item? Where does this item rate in my personal value system?

Do this exercise quietly. When you and a friend have both finished the list, share your answers and discuss any differences.

F. My Personal Values

(Hot-Spot Discussion)

1. Say:

If you really value something, you're willing to talk about the value openly and if necessary to defend your position in the face of questions or opposition. Look at the "Value Indicators" list one more time and select three or four items that you have a strong position on and would be willing to talk about in front of the whole group. Star the items.

2. Give the participants small cards on which to write their first and last names. Collect the cards.

3. Say:

I will draw someone's name from this pack. If your name is picked, you will be on the Hot Spot, and will be asked to explain your position on one of the items you starred. Decide which item you will talk about if your name is picked.

4. Pull a name and ask several questions like:

What item do you want to talk about?

What is your position on ________________________?

Do your peers agree with that position? your parents?

Have you felt that way for a long time or is it something you've come to only recently?

Conclude by asking if anyone else has a question or response for the Hot Spot person.

5. Continue with as many persons as time allows.

Alternate Discussion Technique

1. Move to small dialogue groups.

2. Say:

Each person will have a chance now to find out where the people in your small group stand on an issue of your choice. Take turns around the circle. When it is your turn select one item from the "Value Indicators" list and ask each person in your group to comment on that issue. Explain your own position in response to their comments.

PART TWO

Prayer Capsules

And You Know It's Right
(Opening Talk and Prayer)

Most young people have had little previous experience with retreats. An opening talk like this one helps them understand what to expect and sets the tone of serious prayerfulness required for a good retreat.

A. Preparation

For this capsule you will need:

- a record or tape of "And You Know It's Right" by David Meece (from the album *Count the Cost*, Word Inc., Waco, TX) and the equipment to play it

- a large candle

B. Grouping

Arrange the beanbags or cushions in a large informal circle in the large-group area.

C. Invite the retreatants to join you in the prayer circle. Place a lighted candle in the center of the circle, dim the lights, and give a short talk based on the following script.

Script:

A retreat is a very special time. We step out of the everyday routines of our lives and into a whole new way of thinking and acting. This is definitely not what you're usually doing at this time on this day of the week. You're in a different place, with different people, and doing very different things than you normally would.

What happens during a retreat?

The main thing we do is spend time getting in touch with our own hearts. We ask ourselves: Who am I? Who is this person who lives inside my skin? What's important to me? Whom do I love? What do I really want out of life? We try to get past the masks that we so often hide behind and discover what's going on in our deepest, truest hearts.

And when we get quiet enough and serious enough to pay attention to our hearts, we usually discover that God is living there. Even if we haven't been paying much attention to him, God is there, waiting for us to notice him, wanting us to love him the way he loves us.

Another thing that happens when we listen to our hearts is that we often find out that there are things about the way we've been living that we're not very pleased with. The deepest, truest part of us knows what's right and what's wrong. During a retreat we often discover things about our own lives that we want to change.

I'd like you to listen prayerfully now as Christian rock star David Meece sings about tuning in to the deepest part of you and listening to the very heart of you. (*Play "And You Know It's Right."*)

D. After the song, say:

Close your eyes now and spend a few minutes talking to the God who lives "in the deepest part of you." Tell him how you feel about being on this retreat. (*Pause.*) Ask him to bless you and each person here. (*Pause.*) Thank him for giving you life, and for giving his life for you. (*Pause.*) Offer him your deepest heart this weekend and ask him to open it to his love. (*Pause.*) Amen.

Here I Am, Lord
(Night Prayer)

This prayer experience works very well as a closing prayer on the first night of a retreat. It can also be adapted for use at other times.

A. Preparation

For this capsule you will need:

- a record or tape of "Here I Am, Lord" by Dan Schutte, SJ (from the album *Lord of Light*, NALR) and the equipment to play it

- pencils

- lap pads

- copies of the handout for each participant. For convenience in duplicating, a copy of the handout sheet appears in the Tear-Out Section, page 149.

- a candle for each dialogue group. The candles should be lit before the group gathers.

B. Grouping

Gather in the large-group area. Later the group will break into small groups and go to their "Cozy Corners" areas.

C. Invite the group to sit in a prayer circle. Give out copies of the "Here I Am, Lord" handout, lap pads and pencils. Say:

> The song we are going to play is like a dialogue with Jesus. He speaks the verses and we respond with the chorus. In the song Jesus calls each of us to open our hearts to his people, to care for those who are hurting, those who are lonely, those who are in any kind of need. "Whom can I send," Jesus asks, "to heal my broken world?" Can you respond, "Here I am, Lord. Send me"?
>
> As you listen to the song, write in the heart the names of all the people you hold in your heart, and the people you should hold there. As you write each name say to Jesus, "Here I am, Lord. Help me to love this person the way you want me to."

D. Play "Here I Am, Lord."

E. After the song, say:

> You will be moving back to your cozy corners for the closing part of this prayer. Group leaders, please take one of the lighted candles with you. When you get to your corner, form a close circle sitting on the floor. Then, pass the candle around the circle twice. The first time the candle is passed, each person will tell the group three things: How you felt about this retreat before you came; how you feel about it now; and what you hope will happen in your heart because you are here. The second time, pass the candle in silence. This time, each person is to hold the candle for a few moments while everyone else prays silently for him or her. Pray that the person will receive the special graces he or she needs in order to find God today and to respond lovingly to him.
>
> When everyone has been prayed for, put the candle in the center of your group. Each person is to reach out and touch the base with one hand while you pray together the Our Father.

Footprints in the Sand

This can be used for night prayer on the first night of a retreat, or it can be modified for use on other occasions.

A. Preparation

For this capsule you will need:

- the 45-rpm recording of "Footprints in the Sand" by Edgel Groves, published in 1980 by BGO Records, Inc., 3864 Oak Cliff Ind. Court, Doraville, Georgia 30340. This record has the story version on one side and an instrumental version on the other.

- a lighted candle for each small group. Have the candles arranged on a small table before the participants gather.

- a copy of the "Footprints in the Sand" story for each participant. For convenience in duplicating, a copy of the handout sheet appears in the Tear-Out Section, page 149.

B. Grouping

Gather in the large-group area or another comfortable, prayerful setting. Dim the lights.

C. Meditation Prayer and Song

1. Present a meditation based on the following script.

Script:

Spend a few moments becoming as quiet inside and out as you possibly can. Close your eyes, open your hands on your lap, and be as still as possible. (*Pause.*) After Jesus' resurrection, one of the most important things he wanted his friends to know was that he was still alive, still with them in a very real way even when they could no longer see him. Over and over he told them, "I am always with you!" Down through the ages Christians have learned that Jesus' message is still true. He is here now with us, just as he was with those early disciples. Each of us has to learn how to discover his presence within us. We have to learn how to pay attention to a person who is with us even though we don't see him with our eyes or touch him with our hands.

There is a lovely country song in which Edgel Groves tells how one man discovered that Jesus was always present in his life. You may have heard it before if you ever listen to country stations. Listen to it now and imagine that the story Edgel tells is happening to you.

2. Play the record, beginning with the story side. The sequence on the record is:

Side One: a. chorus

                     b. first verse

                     c. chorus

                     d. second verse

                     e. chorus (twice)

Side Two: f. short instrumental

                     g. chorus

                     h. instrumental interlude—55 seconds

                     i. chorus

                     j. instrumental interlude—55 seconds

                     k. chorus (twice)

Toward the end of the first side the music begins to fade. Speaking loudly enough to be heard over the music, say:

> Think back over your day, your week, your month. Can you find any special moments when you knew Jesus was walking with you? any time he would have carried you? (*Turn the record over and begin to play the other side.*)

3. During the first instrumental interlude (h) lower the volume slightly and say:

> Let's pray now for some of the other people in our lives who need to know that Jesus walks with them, comforts them, carries them. Pray for your mom, your dad, each of your brothers and sisters. Mention each one by name and tell Jesus about the special needs and problems each one has. (*Turn the music back up.*)

During the second instrumental interlude (j) lower the volume slightly and say:

> Think now about your friends at school and work. Imagine Jesus walking with them, loving them, enjoying their nonsense, guiding their choices and decisions. Pray especially for any friend who is having problems or who is in any kind of trouble right now. Pray that he or she will know that Jesus is there caring, supporting, helping, giving strength and courage. (*Turn the music back up.*)

As the chorus begins for the last time (k), lower the volume slightly and say:

> Thank Jesus for walking with you today. Ask him for the strength to live tomorrow well. (*When the music ends, allow a few moments of silence.*)

4. Pass out copies of "Footprints in the Sand" for the participants to keep as reminders.

Scripture Prayer

This activity helps young people use the New Testament to deepen their personal relationship with Jesus.

A. Preparation

For this capsule you will need:

- a copy of the "Scripture Prayer" handout for each participant; cut the sheets apart and assemble the starters so that each person receives one complete set. For convenience in duplicating, a copy of the handout sheet appears in the Tear-Out Section, page 150.
- a bible for each participant
- background music and the equipment to play it

B. Grouping

Begin this capsule by having the participants gather in the large-group area. They will move to "alone" spots next. The activity concludes with the participants in their dialogue groups.

C. Give everyone a bible and a set of the "Scripture Prayer" starters. Say:

Work together to find these 10 passages in the New Testament. Use the prayer starters as bookmarks. Don't read the passages yet.

When all bibles are marked say:

Now take your books and move to a corner of this room where you can be alone. Be sure you are at least six feet away from anyone else and on the other side of the room from your best friend.

D. When all are settled and quiet, give a talk based on the following script.

Script:

Open your books to the New Testament. What you are looking at now is a link to the historical person Jesus of Nazareth. The words in front of you were reported by people who knew Jesus personally, people who saw his miracles, who heard his teachings, who stood under his cross, who touched with their own hands his risen body.

We who live now in the post-Easter time, the time when Jesus lives in the world through us, can come to know Jesus better by lovingly and prayerfully reading these words. When we read the New Testament with faith, it is often possible to experience Jesus speaking directly to our own hearts through the words of scripture.

We are going to try to experience that living word today. When I finish giving the directions, turn to any passage you have marked. Read the passage several times, prayerfully and attentively. Spend some time talking to Jesus about the passage, asking him to tell you what message he wants you to hear in those words. Write his message to you on the marker, and then turn to another passage. It isn't necessary to do all 10 passages. Spend as much time as you can talking with Jesus about any of them.

Quiet your heart now. Ask Jesus to speak to you through the words of his gospel. When your heart is ready, open the bible and begin. (*Play some quiet music as a background to the scripture prayer. Allow 30 to 45 minutes, depending on the prayerfulness of the group.*)

Toward the end of the prayer period say:

Look back over all the passages you have prayed over, and select one or two favorites to share with your small group.

E. Gather in dialogue groups. Say:

Take turns sharing your favorite passage. Explain to your group what personal message those words of scripture held for you today.

Letters To God, Letters From God

Writing a letter to God can be a form of journaling and a form of prayer. It can be used as an activity in itself or as a prayer response to some other activity.

A. Preparation

For this capsule you will need:

- pencils

- lap pads

- background music and the equipment to play it

- "Letter-to-God" and "Letter-From-God" stationery. For convenience in duplicating, a copy of each handout sheet appears in the Tear-Out Section, page 151.

B. Grouping

Gather in a large group to pass out the materials and give instructions. The participants will then move to "alone" spots.

C. Give everyone a copy of the Letter-to-God stationery, a pencil and a lap pad. Then say:

> Sometimes when we find it difficult to keep our minds on prayer, it helps to write our thoughts to God in the form of a letter. Take this paper now and move to a corner of the room where you can be alone. When you are settled, spend the first few minutes just getting in touch with the presence of God within you. Then begin to write. Use the sentence starters around the edge for ideas. Try to write at least one paragraph about each idea. What you write in your letter will be between you and God only; you will not be asked to share it. When you have finished, come to me or another group leader and we will give you your next activity.

Play some quiet background music as the group is writing. When individuals approach you for the second activity, give them the "Letter-From-God" stationery and say:

> On this paper you are going to write God's answer to your letter. First spend some time thinking about these words from the prophet Isaiah. God is speaking to you and saying: "Do not be afraid. You are mine and I love you." Try to really *hear* God saying that to you tonight. Think — what else does God want to say to me? How would he answer the letter I just wrote him? Then write "Dear *(your name)*" on your paper and write a letter from God to you.

Alternative:

a) Tell the group to sign their Letter-to-God anonymously, for example, Troubled in Wisconsin, A Lonely Left-out, Happy to Be Alive. Explain that later their letter will be given to someone here to answer in God's name. They will have to remember how they signed their letter so they will know which answer to claim.

b) Collect all the letters, then give them out again. Make sure no one gets his or her own letter. Give everyone a piece of Letter-From-God stationery and an envelope. Say:

> Reverently read the letter you now have, remembering that it was written to God. Then spend some time praying for the person whose letter you have just read. Ask God to let you know what he wants the person to hear from him tonight. Then answer the letter in God's name. When you have finished, put both letters in the envelope, address it to the original writer, seal it and give it to me.

c) Collect all the letters and give them out at an appropriate time.

Reconciliation With Individual Confession

A retreat provides an excellent opportunity for teen-agers to experience a meaningful celebration of the sacrament of reconciliation. Offering them this opportunity will require some extra planning on your part.

1. Engage the services of several priest confessors, at least one for every 10 retreatants.

2. Plan sufficient time in your schedule to prepare for the sacrament and to allow each person as much time as required for individual confession.

3. Encourage the participants to take advantage of this opportunity either to go to confession or to have a private conference with a priest.

4. Assure privacy for the individual confessions or conferences. Provide at least one confessional with a screen and at least one face-to-face option.

5. Plan meaningful activities to engage the entire group while individual confessions are taking place so that a prayerful atmosphere is maintained throughout.

A. Preparation

For this capsule you will need:

- a slide show based on Psalm 139 (See page 114 for sources of suitable slides.)

- copies of the "Psalm 139" and "Preparation for the Sacrament of Reconciliation" handouts for each participant. You may need other handouts depending on the activities you choose (see Activity E). For convenience in duplicating, a copy of each handout sheet appears in the Tear-Out Section, pages 152-153.

- reflective background music and the equipment to play it

B. Grouping

Begin the session in the large-group area.

C. Why Confession?

Script:

One of the things that is unique about the Catholic church is the sacrament of reconciliation, also called confession. Reconciliation is a sacramental celebration of God's loving mercy. It is an opportunity for us to bring to Jesus our sick and wounded souls so that his love can heal us.

Sin is a powerful factor in our lives. No matter how much we want to be good, we often find ourselves making choices that we know are not according to God's will for us. One sinful choice leads to another until we find that we are caught in a habitual pattern of sin from which we can't seem to escape. Lying to parents, cheating on homework, misuse of alcohol, sexual experimentation, shoplifting, use of foul language—such sinful habits as these seem to take over our lives, sapping our wills of the energy needed to change them.

We can't do it alone. We can't just decide today to change our sinful habits and be new people tomorrow. We can't, but God can. The power of God's grace has changed many lives, and can change each of ours if we are open to that possibility. God works in our lives in many ways. He speaks directly to our hearts, he touches us through the example of our family and friends, he influences us through the writings of scripture and other inspirational books, he teaches us through the leaders of our churches, and he prods us through painful and difficult life experiences. But one of his most powerful means of helping us to overcome our sinfulness is through the sacrament of reconciliation. This sacrament is a face-to-face encounter with God, represented by his priest. As honestly and candidly as possible we open our hearts, acknowledging whatever is offensive to God in them and asking for forgiveness and for the grace of true repentance. And the priest, speaking in the name of God and as a representative of the church, declares our sins forgiven and tells us to go in peace.

Tonight you will have an opportunity to celebrate the sacrament of reconciliation. Many of you may be afraid of that prospect. Some of you may not have been to confession for years. I *strongly encourage* you to go tonight. Confession is one of the seven sacraments of your church and should not be disregarded.

D. Dialogue With the Priest Confessors

Introduce the priest confessors. Ask them if they would be willing to answer a few questions for the group about confession. Then ask the questions below, giving each priest a chance to comment on them. Finally, open the floor for questions from the youth.

Questions:

1. Young people often ask me why they have to go to confession, why they can't just ask God in their hearts for forgiveness. Would you answer that question for them?

2. Sometimes teen-agers worry about talking to the priest about something embarrassing, especially sexual sins. Can you address that worry?

3. If someone goes to confession to you, what happens the next time you meet that person? Do you remember all his or her sins?

4. Would you explain to the group about the seal of confession?

(Now invite the participants to ask any questions they might have about confession.)

E. Explanation of the Reconciliation Process

1. Write on the board (or on a chart) an outline of the next two hours. Say:

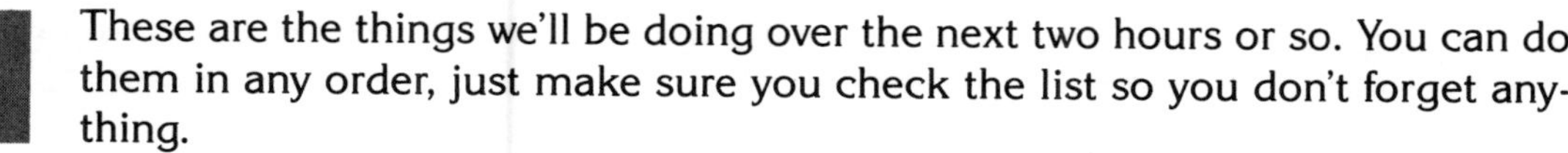

These are the things we'll be doing over the next two hours or so. You can do them in any order, just make sure you check the list so you don't forget anything.

(This is a sample listing. You can add or delete activities depending on your own circumstances. The goal is to keep everyone in a quiet, reflective mood for as long as the individual confessions will take.)

> 1. Examination of Conscience
> 2. Individual Confession
> 3. Letter to God (see p. 151)
> 4. Letter From God (see p. 151)
> 5. One-on-one dialogue with any adult leader (see p. 159)
> 6. One-on-one dialogue with a youth leader (see p. 160)
> 7. *Palanca* notes
> 8. Scripture prayer (see p. 150)

2. Give out copies of the "Preparation for the Sacrament of Reconciliation" handout.

Say:

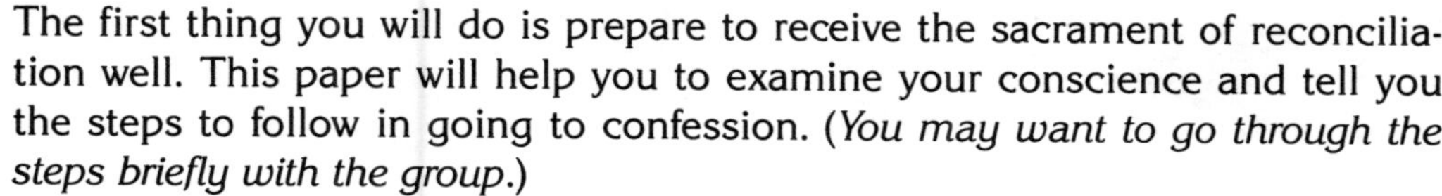

The first thing you will do is prepare to receive the sacrament of reconciliation well. This paper will help you to examine your conscience and tell you the steps to follow in going to confession. (*You may want to go through the steps briefly with the group.*)

3. Tell where each priest will be located and explain the option of kneeling behind the screen or confessing face-to-face. Encourage the young people to try the face-to-face option if they have never done so. Provide one "waiting chair" outside each confession place, and some method of assuring that someone is always waiting to be next. Don't allow the others to queue up at the waiting chair. It is difficult to keep the teen-agers in the queue from chatting and causing a distraction to the persons who are next in line for confession.

4. Give directions for each of the other activities on the list. Pass out the "Psalm 139" handout and any other handouts that will be needed, lap pads and pencils.

F. Sacramental Reconciliation

1. Move to the chapel or prayer room to begin the reconciliation service. Darken the room.

2. Present the slides prepared for Psalm 139, reading the psalm slowly and prayerfully against a backdrop of reflective music.

3. After the slide show, turn the lights on low. Say:

> Spend a few minutes reflecting on the psalm and the response statements found on the handout; then move directly into the examination of conscience and the rest of the reconciliation process.

4. It may take 90 minutes or more for everyone to go to confession and complete the other activities. Keep the process flowing smoothly and, as much as possible, maintain an atmosphere of prayerfulness throughout.

Celebrating Eucharist

The eucharistic celebration can and should be a high point on a retreat. The atmosphere of caring and belonging that has been developed throughout the retreat should culminate naturally in the sacramental sharing at the eucharistic table.

Keep the retreat Mass informal and warm, yet prayerful and reverent. If possible gather in a comfortable space. Use a low table for the altar and arrange floor cushions in an informal semi-circle around it. Provide a chair for the presider.

Involve the young people in as many ways as possible in both the planning and the celebration of the Eucharist. Schedule about 15 to 30 minutes for planning. Assign a small group to each of the tasks listed on the "Mass Preparation" handout sheet. For convenience in duplicating, a copy of the handout sheet appears in the Tear-Out Section, page 154.

PART THREE

Communication Capsules

Ice-Breaking Exercises

A. Preparation

For this capsule you will need the following items at each small-group table:

- a few wideline markers
- a large name tag (about 4″ x 4″) for each person
- pencils
- pins
- small pieces of paper or registration cards in three colors

B. Grouping

Have the participants sit where they choose at the dialogue tables. (This means they will automatically sit according to friendship groups.) Later the group will move to a large-group area, and then back to the dialogue tables.

C. Grouping Papers

Say:

Please take a small piece of paper (or registration card) — boys take a green piece, girls take blue, group leaders take pink. Write your first and last name on the paper and then place it in the center of the table. *(Collect the papers, keeping together those from each group.)*

D. Name Tags

Say:

Please use a wideline marker to print your *first* name on the name tag. *(Allow time.)* Now take a pencil and write or draw the following items on the name tag, on the same side as your name. There will be 10 items.

1. a picture of your favorite childhood toy

2. a picture to stand for your favorite activity

3. a childhood nickname

4. the name of your best friend and a one-word description of him or her

5. the name of an adult you admire

6. draw a teardrop and write next to it the date of the last time you cried

7. draw a hand and write next to it the date of the last year you got spanked

8. draw a key and write next to it the date of the last time you got grounded

9. three words that finish this sentence: "My friends think I'm . . . ."

10. the name of your favorite symbol for God: wind, fire, rock, light, air

(As you dictate these items, walk among the tables, collecting the grouping papers and learning to associate the participants' names with their faces.)

E. Selecting Partners

Say:

Bring your name tag and move to the large-group area. On the way, pair up with someone who was *not* sitting at your table. Sit with that person in the large-group area. Find a partner of the opposite sex if possible. *(Discreetly tell the adults to hold back a minute so they can choose as partners any teen-agers being left out.)*

F. Sharing Name Tag Items

When all are settled say:

Now give your name tag to your partner and take turns explaining the symbols and words to each other. Talk about one item at a time. Listen carefully, because you will be using what you learn about your partner to introduce him or her to the entire group.

(Use this time to create your dialogue groupings for the retreat. See pages 116-117 for grouping techniques.)

G. Introductions

Say:

Look at your partner's name tag again and select the three most interesting items to tell us all about. *(Allow time.)* Now, introduce your partner to the group saying something like: "This is Tom Jones. I just learned that. . . ."

H. Announce Groups

Give the leaders the names of their group members. Have them read off the names and invite their group to a table.

I. Small-group Activity

Once settled at the tables, play the "Simon" name game (p. 93).

Show Your Hand

This is a simple exercise that often generates profound discussions. It can be used to fill an empty 10 minutes or can be extended to an hour or more.

1. Sit at dialogue tables. Say:

I will read aloud some controversial statements. As each is read, tell your group how you feel about the statement by the number of fingers you show on the table:

5 fingers mean you totally agree

4 fingers mean you agree somewhat

3 fingers mean you can't make up your mind

2 fingers mean you disagree somewhat

1 finger means you definitely disagree (Use your pinky, please!)

a fist means pass; you don't want to express your opinion at this time

(Review the code one more time before continuing.)

The process works like this: Everyone puts his or her right fist on the table. I will read a statement and give you a minute to think. Then we will all knock on the table three times counting: one, two, three, show. After the three count, we all show our answers. Ready to try it? Put your right fist on the table. First statement: *Girls and women are more religious then men and boys.* Think a minute. Knock together: One, two, three, show. Now look at everyone's answer and discuss the statement. If someone showed a 1 and someone else a 5, those two should begin by explaining their positions to one another. *(Allow a few minutes for the discussion.)*

2. Continue with statements such as the ones below. Discussion time on each can be longer or shorter depending on the interest of the group.

Women should be allowed to be priests.

Marijuana should be legalized.

My parents trust me.

I want to marry a virgin.

I came tonight because I wanted to.

The legal age for drinking should be 21.

Jesus walked on water.

Priests should be allowed to marry.

If men are drafted, women should be drafted.

Sex should be saved for marriage.

This is boring.

Sunday Mass should be optional.

We each have to decide for ourselves what is right and wrong.

I pray every day.

Drunken drivers should be jailed.

Students who attend a Christian school are more religious than public
school students.

I belong to a "huggy" family.

I like strict teachers.

Families should go to church together on Sunday.

I like winter.

I go to school because I want to.

I go to church because I want to.

Teen-agers should be punished when they misbehave.

I should be punished when I misbehave.

I think of God often.

God punishes me when I'm bad.

I expect to go to heaven when I die.

Jesus is alive right now.

People are basically good.

Jesus is my personal friend.

Lying to teachers is necessary.

Lying to parents is necessary.

My parents trust me.

My parents should trust me.

Teen-agers should have a definite curfew.

Teen-agers who break curfew should be grounded.

Teen-agers with jobs should help pay family expenses.

I really try to make my family happy.

I would allow my *(freshman, sophomore, junior, senior)* son to date.
I would allow my *(freshman, sophomore, junior, senior)* daughter to date.

I willingly do my fair share of the family chores.

Our family discusses problems rationally.

3. You can vary the discussion patterns by saying things like:

This time the oldest person in the group discuss with the youngest *or* This time only the blue-eyed people talk and the browns listen *or* This time everyone explain the meaning of your response.

Cozy Corner Questions

This is an excellent activity for getting the group to share openly and deeply. Allow at least 45 minutes for it; you could spend as long as 90 minutes. The questions work well as a late-night exercise on the opening night of a retreat. Because the teenagers like this activity so much, you might plan to use it twice on one retreat or pick it up as a backup if something else fizzles out.

A. Preparation

For this capsule you will need:

* a copy of the directions for each group leader.   For convenience in duplicating, a copy of the directions appears in the Tear-Out Section, page 155.

* one set of questions for each dialogue group. For convenience in duplicating, the questions appear in the Tear-Out Section, pages 156-158. Prepare the questions as follows:

  1) put stars on the backs of the cards to correspond with the stars printed on the faces of the cards

  2) put a piece of clear contact paper on the front and back of each page (optional)

  3) cut the questions apart and put each set of 36 questions in an envelope

B. Grouping

Assign each small group to a "cozy corner" — a comfortable spot where the participants can sit around in a circle on floor pillows or couches.

C. Cozy Corner Activity

Give each group leader a set of cards and a copy of the directions. Assign a closing time.

One-on-One Dialogues With Group Leaders

This can be a very beautiful experience for your group leaders as well as for the young people. It is a chance for each teen-ager to speak privately to an adult leader and a youth leader. A set of questions is provided for the leaders. These should be used merely as suggestions; the dialogue should be guided mainly by the interests and needs of each teen being spoken to.

A. Preparation

For this capsule you will need:

- copies of the adult and youth leader directions. For convenience in duplicating, a copy of each handout sheet appears in the Tear-Out Section, pages 159-160.

- copies of the prayers for each person (give these to the youth leaders to distribute). For convenience in duplicating, a copy of each handout sheet appears in the Tear-Out Section, page 161.

B. Grouping

Arrange the room so each leader has a somewhat private space for the one-on-one dialogues. Set up each dialogue space with two chairs or beanbags and a lighted candle. Dim the lights.

C. Dialogues

Explain that the young people are free to approach any leader, not necessarily their table group leader. The conferences should last about 5-10 minutes. If someone needs longer counseling for a specific problem, he or she should arrange another time for that with the leader.

Maintain an atmosphere of quiet reflection throughout the time of the conferences. Provide quiet activities that will keep everyone occupied.

If both adult and youth leaders are available, encourage the participants to have a conference with one of each.

Ask God*

This technique works especially well with teen-agers who have lots of questions about God and religious matters.

A. Preparation

For this capsule you will need:

- six participants, a combination of leaders and teen-agers (Select bright, articulate volunteers.) Tell three of the six that in the next activity they will be playing the role of God. They should decide among themselves which person of the Trinity each will play. The other three volunteers will be God's interrogators. They should think of some good questions that they've always wanted to ask God.

- (optional) the Insight film, "God in the Dock," and the equipment to show it. The film can be rented from Audience Planners, 5107 Douglas Fir Road, Calabasas, CA 91302 (800-624-8613) or purchased from Paulist Productions, P.O. Box 1057, Pacific Palisades, CA 90272 (213-454-0688).

B. Grouping

Gather in the large-group area. Seat the "Trinity" on three chairs in the center of the group. Seat the interrogators on three chairs facing them.

C. Play

Have an interrogator begin by addressing a question to any of the three persons, or to God in general. If the question is addressed to God in general, the three will have to confer before answering. Say:

> Anyone who doesn't like God's answer to a question, or who just wants a chance to play God, can at any time tap one of the three on the shoulder and take that person's chair. Anyone who wants to ask God a question can tap an interrogator on the shoulder and take his or her chair.

D. Director's Role

You may need to move into an interrogator's chair in the beginning to get some good questions going. If a heretical answer is being proposed by "God," move into a God-chair to straighten out the error.

E. As a follow-up to this activity, you may want to show the film "God in the Dock." This is a sophisticated version of the above activity.

---

*This activity was created by Gerry Fischer, a staff member at the TYME OUT Center.

Jesus Interview

This activity helps the teen-agers to be more conscious of the presence of Jesus in their everyday world and to imagine how their friends, family, community and world must look in his eyes.

A. Preparation

For this capsule you will need:

- five or six copies of the "Jesus Interview" questions. For convenience in duplicating, a copy of the handout appears in the Tear-Out Section, pages 162-163. Cut the questions apart and assemble them so that each person receives three or four different questions.
- a volunteer (youth or adult) to "play Jesus" in the upcoming interview.
- a microphone and tape recorder (or a video camera, if available)

B. Grouping

This activity takes place in the large-group area.

C. Reflection Time

Say:

Yesterday I received a phone call from station HVEN. They are sending over a celebrity to interview some of us for a special on tonight's news. Most of you have probably heard of the celebrity, his formal name is Jesus Christ, but his friends usually call him JC. The station wants us to be well-prepared for the interview so they've sent over a set of questions like those he'll probably ask. *(Give everyone a pack of questions.)* I'm giving each of you some of the questions to prepare. Spend the next 20 minutes or so thinking about your questions and jotting down things you might say to answer them. You may work in groups of two or three if you wish.

D. The Interview

Bring in "Jesus" with his microphone and tape recorder (or use a video camera). Have Jesus walk among the group Phil Donahue style, asking questions like those the students have reflected upon.

Love Letters From Home

Giving each retreatant a love letter from his or her parents is a powerful retreat experience. If you choose to do this activity, it is *imperative* that every young person receive a letter. This may require many phone calls on your part.

A. Preparation

For this capsule you will need:

- a letter for each teen-ager

    About three or four weeks before the retreat, send the parents a letter explaining the love letter idea and its importance. Tell the parents that the letters should be kept secret. Have the letters returned to you well before the retreat.

    Check the letters against your list as they arrive. Make *sure* you get one for everyone. If you do not, don't plan on this activity. Instead, give out the letters that you have received *privately* toward the end of the retreat and ask the participants to read them at home.

- stationery, envelopes and a candle in a glass holder for each group. Have the leaders pick these up along with the letters for their groups.

- a tape or record of "Arms of Love" by Amy Grant (from the album *Age to Age*, Word, Inc., Waco, Texas) and the equipment to play it

- (optional) slides of children being treated lovingly by their parents, and a projector

B. Grouping

Have the participants gather in the prayer space with each small group sitting together in a circle on the floor. The area should be large enough for the participants to move to "alone" spots to read and respond to their letters.

C. Prayer Service

Have the leaders put the lighted candle and the letters in the center of their circle. Put the letters face down so the names don't show.

Say:

Our God is a loving God, but most of us have a hard time learning to believe that. We're not sure that he loves *me*. The best way God has of teaching us about his love for us is through the loving people he sends into our lives. And for most of us, the most loving people of all are our parents.

I'd like you to spend a moment thinking of all the loving your parents have given you over the years. Draw pictures in your memory: your mom hugging you when you were hurt or afraid; your dad carrying you on his shoulders; sitting in your dad's lap as he read you a book; running in after school to tell your mom you won your first baseball game. See if you can remember yourself being loved at each stage of your growing up. *(Pause.)*

Optional:

At this time show slides of children being treated lovingly by their parents. If possible, obtain such slides of the members of your group when they were children.

Say:

I'm going to play a song now by Christian rock singer, Amy Grant. *(Show the picture on the* Age to Age *album.)* Amy uses images of a loving parent to talk about her relationship with God. She sees herself as a little child held by God "in the arms of love." As you listen to the song, close your eyes and try to imagine that you, too, are a little child and that God is holding you in his arms.

After the song say:

Our parents are the first to teach us about love, but they are often the hardest people for us to learn to love well. Tonight we have a special gift for you — a love letter from your parents. Your group leaders will give out the letters and some stationery and envelopes. Go off by yourself to read your letters and to answer them. When you're finished, seal your answer, address it, and hand it in. We'll stamp the letters and mail them. *(Play "Arms of Love" again as the letters are being distributed.)*

Alternative:

It is possible—and valuable—to have the young people write a letter *to* their parents even if you did not do the letters-from-parents part of this exercise. It will require more motivation, however.

God Questions

This makes an excellent exercise to use with a mixed group of youth and adults, for example, a parent-youth retreat. It can also be used in many other settings.

A. Preparation

For this capsule you will need:

- copies of the handout sheet for each participant. For convenience in duplicating, a copy of the handout sheet appears in the Tear-Out Section, page 164.

B. Grouping

Set up chairs for half the group in a circle all around the outside of the large-group area. Set up another circle of chairs facing them. For the follow-up activity, you will need a small-group area.

C. Knee-to-Knee Dialogue

1. Ask all the girls to sit on the outside chairs, facing a boy, and all the boys to sit on the inside chairs, facing a girl. (Use the adults in either inside or outside chairs to even off the sets.)

2. Say:

One way we can realize how much we've grown in our faith understanding is to remember how we thought about things when we were little children. So dig back into your memory bank now and tell your partner what you thought God looked like when you were a little child. The outside person answer first, then the inside person. *(Allow time for both answers.)* Then say: How has your idea of God changed? What kind of mental image do you use for God now? Do you think of God in human form? Do you have separate images for Jesus and for God the Father? Is your God male or female or androgynous? *(Allow time for the answers.)*

3. Say:

Everyone in the outside circle stand and move three chairs to the right. *(Wait till all are relocated.)* Say:

Tell your new partner what the "little-kid you" thought God's job was. What did you think God did all day up there in heaven? This time the inside person answers first. *(Allow time for the answers.)* Then say: And now what do you think God's job is? What role does God play in human life? When we pray for people who are sick, does God make them better? Does he give the farmers rain when they pray for it? When Notre Dame plays USC and both teams are praying to win, does God choose sides? *(Allow time for the answers.)*

4. Say:

Now it's the inside circle's turn to move three chairs to the right. *(Continue in this manner for each of the following sets of questions. Always ask a THEN question and allow time for the answers, then ask a NOW question.)*

THEN Question:

Tell your partner about your childhood ideas of right and wrong. How did you know good from bad? What kind of discipline did your parents use? Was it effective?

NOW Question:

Where do you look for moral guidance in your life today? Do you still follow your parents' moral teachings? Should you? In your opinion, are most people basically good or basically evil?

THEN Question:

Describe for your partner your childhood ideas of heaven and hell.

NOW Questions:

What do you believe now about life after death? How do you understand heaven and hell? Do you plan on going to heaven someday? Do you know anyone who you are sure is now in heaven? in hell?

THEN Question:

When you were a child, what prayers did you say? Did you pray as a family? What's your earliest memory of really praying for something?

NOW Question:

How do you pray now? When and where? Do you pray formula prayers or do you use your own words? Do you have a sense of God's presence when you pray? Do you think he really listens and cares?

When all are finished say:

Now return to your dialogue tables.

D. Small-group Dialogue

l. Give everyone a copy of the "God Questions" handout. Say:

This paper contains a list of questions like those we were just dealing with. Read the questions through silently and mark with a P any question that is a PROBLEM to you right now in your life. *(Allow time.)*

2. Say:

Take turns around the circle. When it is your turn, select one of your problem areas. Ask whether anyone else also has that area marked. Then spend some time as a table discussing the question. If you come upon a particularly thorny problem and would like it to be brought up in the entire group, let me know when I come around.

3. Circulate among the tables. If any table wants a question brought to the larger assembly, do that at the end of the discussion time or set another time if there are many questions.

PART FOUR

Game Capsules

Fun should be an integral part of all youth ministry activities. Nothing is quite as effective as laughter for building a group of strangers into a community of friends. This section contains 11 games that the teen-agers we have worked with especially enjoyed. Other game sources are listed at the end of this section.

Simon

1. Have the participants sit in small groups or teams.

2. Say:

You probably have played with the electronic game called Simon. This is a getting-to-know-you game based on the Simon game; our version uses names instead of colors. The person closest to me in each circle please raise your hand. You will begin the game. You say your name and the name of anyone across the circle from you (Jenny . . . Jeff). Jeff repeats the two names and adds another name from your group (Jenny . . . Jeff . . . Karen). Karen repeats the three names and adds a fourth, and so on. When you've used all the names once, start to use them a second time. Your aim is to make the list as long as possible without making a mistake. When someone breaks the sequence, the whole team makes a buzzing sound (as the Simon game does). The person who made the mistake will then begin a new round, saying just his or her name and the name of one other person.

3. After five or 10 minutes call a halt to the game. Determine the winner by finding out which group had the longest string of names.

My Aunt Sally IQ Test

1. Say:

This is a test of the IQs of the members of this group. We have to find out if you're smart enough to handle the heavy thinking we'll be doing. All you have to do to pass the test is repeat one little phrase exactly as I say it. Now watch. My Aunt Sally has five fat dogs and seven scrawny cats. *(Say the phrase with elaborate gestures and exaggerated expression.)*

2. Call on various people to try the test. No matter how well they mimic you, they pass only if they say the words "Now watch" before repeating the phrase!

Moon Pennies

1. Say:

This game is a brain teaser. All you have to do to win is discover what you can buy with moon pennies. When you know, don't tell anyone how you know. Some people might not figure it out all weekend. I've known people to go on for weeks trying to discover the moon pennies secret.

2. Give some starter clues like these:

Moon pennies will buy apples but they won't buy oranges.

Moon pennies will buy puppies but not dogs, kittens but not cats.

You can trade moon pennies for dollars but not for dimes or quarters.

You can give moon pennies to Colleen but not to June, to Matt but not to Fred.

One of the best things to buy with moon pennies is a little yellow balloon, but you can't buy a big multicolor poster.

3. Then say:

Go around the group now. Each person ask me a question about what to buy; for example, "Can I buy pepper?" (Yes) The next person might ask, "Can I buy salt?" (No)

When you've solved the mystery, make a statement instead of asking a question. Say something like: "You can keep moon pennies in glasses but not in jars." or "You can save moon pennies for a week but not for a day or month." Don't tell anyone the secret. Just keep giving more clues.

*(If **you** still haven't discovered the secret, moon pennies buy anything that has a double letter in it.)*

Unmusical Chairs

1. Arrange the chairs in a circle. There should be one chair for each person except you.

2. Stand in the center of the circle and say:

This game is called unmusical chairs. The person standing in the center is IT and says something like this: "If you kissed your mom good-by before the retreat, stand," or "Everyone who has a bank account, stand." When IT says "Go," the people who are standing all scramble for a different seat. The person who doesn't get a chair is the next IT.

Remember these three things:

1) Don't move until IT says "Go."

2) Always move at least two chairs away from where you are presently sitting.

3) Whoever is first to touch a chair gets to sit there.

3. Start the game by saying:

If you ever got a D on your report card, stand. *(Pause.)* Go!

Team Scrabble

1. Make a set of Scrabble letters on stiff cards about 3″ x 4″. Look at a Scrabble board to determine how many letters to make and the point value of each. You might want to make a scoreboard to report the results of the game.

2. Provide at least one good dictionary or Scrabble word list.

3. Ask the participants to sit in small groups at tables or in circles on the floor.

4. Spread the letters face down on a table in the center of the room. Have each group send a runner to pick up 10 letters. Tell them to keep the letters face down till you say "Go!"

5. Each team makes words as in a Scrabble game, using letters both horizontally and vertically. The usual Scrabble rules apply: no proper names, no abbreviations, and so forth.

6. When the first group is finished, allow one more minute and then call time.

7. Ask each table to send one or two people to be checkers at a neighboring table. You—and the dictionary—will be the final judge on disputed words. The checkers count the score and report it to you at the scoreboard.

8. For the next round, have runners return the original letters to the pile and pick 10 more. *(Watch this process closely to prevent peeking at letters.)*

9. Play as many rounds as you have time for.

Scripture Acronym Game

1. Have the participants sit in the large-group area. Be sure everyone can see the chalkboard.

2. Choose one of the passages below—or any other short scripture passage. Write the first letter of each word *down* the chalkboard. Gradually fill in the words of the passage, starting with the articles and prepositions. Keep the best clue words till last.

3. The first person to identify the passage *exactly* wins.

Alternative:

Work in teams writing the answers on long strips of paper. The first team to bring you the exact wording of the passage wins.

Scripture Passages*

- Love your neighbor as yourself.   (Mt 19:19)
- Give us today our daily bread.   (Mt 6:11)
- The last shall be first, and the first shall be last.   (Mt 20:16)
- Where your treasure is, there your heart is also.   (Mt 6:21)
- Learn from me, for I am gentle and humble of heart.   (Mt 11:29)
- Come and follow me.   (Mk 10:21)
- Make ready the way of the Lord.   (Mk 1:3)
- Come after me and I will make you fishers of men.   (Mt 4:19)
- Let the children come to me.   (Mt 19:14)
- How blest are the poor in spirit: the reign of God is theirs.   (Mt 5:3)
- When a person strikes you on the right cheek, turn and offer him the other.   (Mt 5:39)
- Love your enemies, do good to those who hate you.   (Lk 6:27)
- Blest too the peacemakers; they shall be called sons of God.   (Mt 5:9)
- Who can this be that the wind and the sea obey him?   (Mk 4:41)
- If I just touch his clothing I shall get well. (Mt 5:28)
- The harvest is good but laborers are scarce.   (Mt 9:37)
- Come to me, all you who are weary.   (Mt 11:28)
- It is I; do not be afraid!   (Mt 14:27)
- You are "Rock," and on this rock I will build my church.   (Mt 16:18)
- Give to Caesar what is Caesar's, but give to God what is God's.   (Lk 20:25)

---

* These quotations are from the *New American Bible.* If your group is more familiar with another translation, use the wording from that version.

Pocket, Purse and Person Scavenger

1. Divide the group into even-numbered teams. If some groups are short one person, have them designate in advance someone who will always be counted twice.

2. Have the group decide on a team name. Record the names of the teams across the top of the chalkboard.

3. Call out items like those listed below. The items must already be present at the table—in pockets or purses or on the persons. Record the scores on the chalkboard.

Say:

I will give your team one point for each button on your clothing. The button must have a buttonhole to be counted. *(Pause.)*

The person with the holiest sock will win 25 points for his or her team. *(Pause.)*

Fifty points for the team that can produce the oldest penny. *(Pause.)*

Continue with the following:

1 point for each belt loop

3 points for each stick of unchewed gum

5 points for each pair of non-jeans

25 points for the smallest shoe

25 points for the largest shoe

3 points for each lipstick or chapstick

25 points for the widest hand spread

2 points for each living brother or sister (not counting yourself)

50 points for the longest single shoelace

5 points for each digital watch

5 points for each pair of glasses (not contacts)

10 points for each February birthday

25 points for the longest belt

5 points for each piece of religious jewelry

50 points for the longest strand of hair

1 point for each letter in your last name

25 points for the oldest person present

1 point for each letter printed on a shirt; labels and buttons don't count. *(Do this one last, especially if someone is wearing a shirt with lots of letters on it.)*

Puzzle Cards

1. Create a set of puzzle cards using the puzzles on pages 165-166. Number the cards as shown. (You may prefer to copy the puzzles onto large cards. I use 6″ x 8″ cards.)

2. Give each group a sheet of paper. Tell the groups to appoint a secretary who will number the paper from 1 to 40.

3. Divide the cards into as many packs as you have groups.

4. Put a pack of cards face down on each table. Say:

On each of these cards you will find a number and a puzzle which stands for a common word or phrase. When I say "Go," turn the pack over, spread the cards out on your table and try to figure out the puzzles. When you know an answer, tell your secretary the number and the answer. Work quietly so you don't give your answers away to the other tables. When you finish the whole set, raise your hand.

5. When one group finishes, call "30 seconds." After the 30 seconds, say:

Pack up your cards and pass them to the next table. (*Establish a pattern for rotating the cards.*)

6. When all the groups have had all the cards, read the answers aloud. The table with the most correct answers wins.

Answers:

1.	paradise	21.	tricycle
2.	backward glance	22.	broken off or cut off
3.	long underwear	23.	he's beside himself
4.	see-through blouse	24.	side by side
5.	look around you	25.	man overboard
6.	paradox or paramedics	26.	double cross or tea for two
7.	reading between the lines	27.	Lucille Ball
8.	check up	28.	black-and-white TV
9.	mind over matter	29.	split pea soup
10.	touchdown	30.	son of a gun
11.	split level or bi-level	31.	little house on the prairie
12.	crossroads	32.	equal rights
13.	Oh, gross!	33.	sleeping on the job
14.	neon light	34.	scrambled eggs
15.	high chair	35.	four degrees below zero
16.	downtown	36.	no room in the inn
17.	sandbox	37.	search high and low
18.	six feet underground	38.	quarterback sack
19.	double date	39.	three blind mice
20.	I understand	40.	Count Dracula

Word Scramble

1. Create a set of cards about 2″x 8″, putting a scrambled word on each card (see examples below). Number the cards as shown. (There is an arrow on each word which indicates where the word begins. Do *not* tell your group this. Let the participants figure it out for themselves.)

2. Give each group a sheet of paper. Tell the groups to appoint a secretary who will number the paper from 1 to 40.

3. Divide the cards into as many packs as you have groups.

4. Put a pack of cards face down on each table. Say:

> On each of these cards you will find a number and scrambled letters which can be recombined to form a common word. When I say "Go," turn the pack over, spread the cards out on your table and try to figure out the words. When you know an answer, tell your secretary the number and the answer. Work quietly so you don't give your answers away to the other tables. When you finish the whole set, raise your hand.

5. When one group finishes, call "30 seconds." After the 30 seconds, say:

> Pack up your cards and pass them to the next table. *(Establish a pattern for rotating the cards.)*

6. When all the groups have had all the cards, read the answers aloud. The table with the most correct answers wins.

The following words are particularly appropriate for a confirmation group. You may want to substitute other words to fit the theme you are presenting.

1.	HTACCOIL	CATHOLIC
2.	GONGLIBNE	BELONGING
3.	VRCEISE	SERVICE
4.	TAFIH	FAITH
5.	IIIINNTTAO	INITIATION
6.	TRABCEILEON	CELEBRATION
7.	HCRTSIAEU	EUCHARIST
8.	WONKDEEGL	KNOWLEDGE
9.	ROUACGE	COURAGE
10.	VEEEERRCN	REVERENCE
11.	TAPBMSI	BAPTISM

12.	GRNNNAUEDDTIS	UNDERSTANDING
13.	ODISWM	WISDOM
14.	SIRHMCA	CHARISM
15.	TINNAOIGN	ANOINTING
16.	YOHL RIITPS	HOLY SPIRIT
17.	NOSSROP	SPONSOR
18.	NICYTUMMO	COMMUNITY
20.	TSCNAIIHR	CHRISTIAN
20.	FANOOCNMRIIT	CONFIRMATION
21.	TERUPCRIS	SCRIPTURE
22.	SIINOECD	DECISION
23.	DDTCAANEI	CANDIDATE
24.	PIBHOS	BISHOP
25.	NIIYTTR	TRINITY
26.	NAARICNNOTI	INCARNATION
27.	CEEIOSD	DIOCESE
28.	LOIIGRNE	RELIGION
29.	RHHUCC	CHURCH
30.	GULYRIT	LITURGY
31.	SSUEJ SIHTCR	JESUS CHRIST
32.	MMMTTOCIEN	COMMITMENT
33.	LOIIOGABTN	OBLIGATION
34.	OVMTTIIAON	MOTIVATION
35.	LODETNEVEPM	DEVELOPMENT
36.	RYTOMILA	MORALITY
37.	BYMLOS	SYMBOL
38.	CCNNOOIIITALER	RECONCILIATION
39.	SSEEHPNIA	EPHESIANS
40.	SNAIHTNIROC	CORINTHIANS

Broom Hockey

1. Play this game in an open room with a smooth floor. You will need two brooms, a piece of cloth, masking tape (to establish goal lines) and a scoreboard.

2. Define the court using the masking tape. Goal lines should be about one yard from each end of your playing space. Determine the center of the court and mark it with an X.

3. Place the cloth on the X and the two brooms facing opposite directions on either side of it. Your court should look like this:

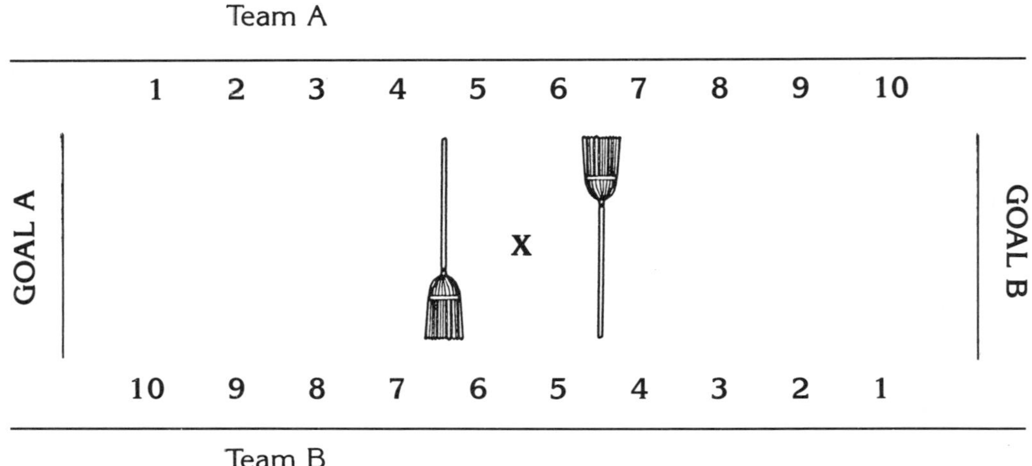

4. Divide the group into two equal teams. The teams stand on opposing sidelines, facing each other.

5. Have the teams count off in opposite directions. (If you have 20 players, Number 1 from Team A and Number 10 from Team B will be facing each other.)

6. Call a number. Both players who have that number run to the center, grab a broom, and try to sweep the rag across the opponent's goal line. The first player to get it over the line wins a point.

7. Keep playing until all the numbers have been called at least once.

Wink

1. Have the girls sit in a circle on chairs. There should be one extra chair. One boy stands behind each chair, including the empty one. Tell the boys to keep their hands clasped behind their backs.

2. The boy with the empty chair winks at one of the girls. She has to leave her chair and run to his before the boy behind her tags her.

3. After a few rounds, switch places so the boys are on the chairs and the girls are winking.

Appendix

Weekend Retreat
(A Sample Schedule)

This retreat plan assumes that there are two directors who have planned the retreat, and a group of five or six adults who have come with the youth as group leaders.

Theme: Persons Are Gifts

FRIDAY PM

7:00 Introductory Exercises

- As the participants arrive, have them pile their sleeping bags and suitcases in the corridor and go directly to the tables.

- Give out registration cards and name tags, and proceed with the activities explained in Activities D-G of "Ice-Breaking Exercises," page 77:
  — Name tags with key words and symbols
  — Sharing with partners
  — Introductions

7:45 Dorms

- Director A: Take the group leaders to the dorm. Give each one the name cards for his or her small group and a copy of "Notes to Group Leaders" (see sample, p. 120). Explain your expectations for the retreat. Call Director B when ready.

- Director B: Play the games, "My Aunt Sally" and "Moon Pennies," pages 93-94, until Director A calls. Then direct the teen-agers to take their gear to the dorms and unpack. In the meantime, prepare the setting for the opening talk and prayer.

8:00 Opening Talk and Prayer

- Sit in a circle for the opening talk and prayer, "And You Know It's Right," page 63.

- Present the rules and regulations for the retreat. (See pages 118-119 for a sample.)

- Have the group leaders call off the names of the persons in their group and move to the discussion tables.

- Play the "Simon" game, page 93.

8:30 Persons Are Gifts

• Give out the "Persons Are Gifts" handouts (p. 138), the memory book covers and the brads (see p. 15).

• Begin with Capsule F, "The Gifts You Have and Are," pages 40-41.

• Read the poem, following the directions in C, page 38.

• Do Capsule D, "The Outside Wrapping vs. the Inside Gift." Share in table groups.

9:30 Gift Wrapping Session

• See page 41, Capsule G, for wrapping the boxes.

• Allow time for everyone to select a box and wrap it. Display the wrapped boxes prominently for the remainder of the retreat. They will be used later.

• Before the break, assign each group to a cozy corner (see p. 14).

10:00 Snack and Break

• Provide a plentiful snack.

• If a gym is available, encourage the participants to play some energy-burning team games like volleyball or basketball. If you don't have a gym, play one or two organized games like "Broom Hockey" and "Wink" (see pp. 102-103); then give the group free time.

• During the break explain the next activity to the group leaders and give them the question cards.

11:00 Cozy Corner Questions

• Gather the participants in small groups for the Cozy Corner questions, pages 156-158. Walk around to be sure each group is comfortable and understands the process for the activity.

11:45 Last-Chance Break

• Allow a 15-minute break. Tell the group that this is the last chance for a snack, soda or smoke before going to bed.

• During the break, prepare the setting for night prayer.

12:00 Night Prayer

• Have the participants gather in the prayer room. Give out the "Here I Am" handouts (p. 149), pencils and lap pads.

• Before beginning night prayer, remind the group of the dormitory rules and of breakfast time (see sample, p. 118).

12:45 Lights Out

- Before retiring, check to be sure the candles are all extinguished, the doors securely locked, and the lights out in the center.

- Get a good night's sleep! Leave the discipline in the dorms to the group leaders. Sleep in an area where you will not be disturbed if the teen-agers misbehave during the night. (Of course, *your* teen-agers will not misbehave!)

SATURDAY AM

8:30 Breakfast

- The groups help with table serving, clean-up, dishes, and so on, as assigned.

- After breakfast, arrange the chairs in the center in a circle for the activity below.

- Prepare the materials needed for the "Trust Walk."

9:15 Morning Prayer and Wake-up Games

- Have the participants sit in a large circle. Call them to prayerful quiet, say a few words about being open to God and to one another today, then play again "Here I Am, Lord."

- Play the game "Unmusical Chairs" (p. 95).

9:45 Trust Walk

- While still in the large circle, give out the blindfolds for the "Trust Walk." Proceed as explained on page 54, Capsules C and D. Do the sharing on the reflection sheet in small groups rather than in a large group as suggested in the manual.

10:45 Team Scrabble

- Play a few rounds of "Team Scrabble" (p. 96).

11:00 Short Break

11:15 Value Systems

- Have the participants gather in the large-group presentation space.

- Give out the "Value Systems" handouts (pp. 147-148) and proceed as explained on page 57.

12:30 Lunch and Long Break

2:00 Puzzle Cards

- Have the participants gather at the small-group tables for the "Puzzle Cards" game (p. 99).

2:15 Scripture Prayer

- Give out bibles and "Prayer Starters." Do the "Scripture Prayer" activity explained on page 68.

3:30 Short Break

- During the break prepare the video for the next activity.

3:45 The Wrapping Is Not the Gift — Video and Discussion

- Have the participants gather in the large-group presentation space. They should bring with them the "Persons Are Gifts" handout and a pencil.

- Show the first 30 minutes of the video "The Heart Has Its Reasons" and do the exercise explained in Capsule H of "Persons Are Gifts" (p. 43).

5:30 Dinner and Long Break

- During the break prepare all the materials you will need for the reconciliation process.

6:45 Leaders' Meeting

- Meet with the group leaders to explain their role in the reconciliation process. Give them the "One-on-One Dialogue" papers and explain them.

7:00 Scavenger Game

- Have the participants gather in table groups. Play "Pocket, Purse and Person Scavenger," page 98.

7:30 Reconciliation Process, One-on-One Dialogues, Letters to God

- Move to the large-group presentation area.

- Follow the procedures for "Sacramental Reconciliation" explained on page 152.

10:00 (Or whenever confessions are finished) Break and Snack

- During the break, gather the group leaders privately. Give them the love letters for their group and the stationery for answering them.

10:45 Love Letters

- Have the participants gather in the prayer space sitting in small-group circles on the floor with their group leaders.

- Do the "Love Letters Prayer Service," pages 85-86.

- Ask the leaders to give out the letters from home and the stationery and envelopes for answering them.

- Have the participants spread around the area to read their letters and answer them.

11:45 Last Chance Break

12:00 Night Prayer

- Ask the participants to gather in the prayer space, bringing their memory books.

- Remind the group about conduct in the dorm. Tell them the procedures for stripping beds and packing up in the morning.

- Lead the closing night prayer that is presented in "Trust Walk," Capsule E, page 55. The closing prayer is on the "Trust Walk" handout, page 146.

12:45 Lights Out

SUNDAY AM

8:30 Breakfast

9:15 Meditation

- Give out the handouts for "Luke 19" (p. 133). The participants will need this handout, a lap pad and a pencil as they move to the "alone" spots for the meditation experience.

- Direct the meditation and reflection as explained on pages 25-27.

10:00 Affirmation

- After the meditation, explain the directions for "With Love From . . . ," Capsule I (p. 43).

- Have the participants take their gift boxes and move to the "cozy corners."

- After the activity, put the gift boxes back in the prayer space.

10:45 Break

11:00 Prepare for Mass

- Gather in table groups.

- Give each table one or two "Mass Preparation" handouts (p. 154) and assign the tasks to the groups. You might want to ask one volunteer from each table to be in the group that prepares the music.

11:30 Eucharistic Celebration

12:30 Lunch

- During the break assemble the materials needed for the clean-up project.

1:00 Evaluation and Clean-up

- Have the participants gather in table groups.

- Give each participant a half sheet of paper. Ask them to write you a short note evaluating the retreat. Encourage them to sign the notes. Ask the group leaders to collect the notes and give them to you.

- While they are writing, go from table to table assigning and explaining the clean-up jobs. Give each group one section of the retreat area to attend to.

- Prepare the prayer space for the closing activity. You will need the gift boxes (arranged on the altar) and two candles.

1:30 Closing Prayer

- Ask the participants to gather in the prayer space, bringing their memory booklets and a pencil.

- Do the "Closing Prayer," Capsule J (p. 44) from "Persons Are Gifts."

2:00 Dismissal

Music

Many of the TYME CAPSULES activities require the use of recorded music. I find that contemporary Christian rock music works well with young people. Much of this music is available from

> Word, Inc.
> Waco, Texas

Individual songs are suggested in the capsules.

For on-going information on the use of secular rock music with youth groups, subscribe to Father Don Kimball's excellent publication

> Top Music Countdown
> Cornerstone Media, Inc.
> P.O. Box 6236
> Santa Rosa, CA 95406

Many of the activities, especially the meditation exercises, call for gentle background music. Some sources of background music include

> *Reflections* and *Reflections II* (the Dameans)
> NALR
> 10802 N. 23rd Ave.
> Phoenix, AZ 85029

> A series of *Healing Music* tapes (Steve Halpern, Daniel Kobialka, and Georgia Kelly)
> Credence Cassettes
> 115 E. Armour Blvd.
> P.O. Box 40291
> Kansas City, MO 64141

> *Songs of the Seashore* (flutist James Galway)
> RCA

> *Rosewood and Silver* (Koenig and Weisbach)
> Westwood Recording Studios
> 964 W. Grant Road
> Tuscon, AZ 85705

Slides

Today's young people are visually oriented. Presentations and prayer experiences can often be enhanced by slides. Begin to acquire a set of slides featuring the members of your group and local events. Sets of slides on a variety of topics are also available commercially.

Images of Life, a slide package containing 300 slides and 30 slide programs in a 3-ring binder.

The Center for Learning
P.O. Box 910
Villa Maria, PA 16155

Visual Meditations, slide packages on a variety of themes with accompanying scripts and audio tapes.

The Liturgical Press
St. John Abbey
Collegeville, MN 56321

Game Books

It is impossible to credit the authors of games such as the ones given in this book. Games that work catch on quickly and undergo numerous modifications. As far as I know, I made up the Simon game. The others I picked up either by playing them or by reading a version in a game book.

The following are my favorite game books:

The New Games Book (about $5.00) by Andrew Fluegelman (Garden City, N.Y.: Doubleday and Co., 1976) can be purchased from

> New Games Foundation
> P.O. Box 7091
> San Francisco, CA 94120

Also *More New Games*.

Fun 'n' Games (about $5.00) by Rice, Rydberg, and Yaconelli is available from

> Zondervan Publishing House
> 1415 Lake Drive, S.E.
> Grand Rapids, MI 49506

Ideas (four volumes for $21.95), published quarterly, can be ordered from

> Youth Specialities
> 1224 Greenfield Drive
> El Cajon, CA 92021

Encyclopedia of Serendipity ($15.00) and other Serendipity books are available from

> SERENDIPITY,
> Box 1012
> Littleton, CO 80160

Grouping Methods

Name tags   If you know ahead of time who will be attending the session, you can use name tags to designate the groups.

- Before the session make a name tag for each participant, youth and adult.

- Put the name tags in groups of eight, determining the distribution you want in each group.

- Put a group symbol (number, letter, sign) on each name tag in each pack; put a corresponding symbol at each table.

- Make a list of the members of each group to give to the group leaders.

- Put all the name tags back in alphabetical order so they will be easy for the participants to pick up.

- As participants arrive, ask them to sit at the table marked with their symbol.

Friendship-group distribution   This is my favorite method for establishing new groups for a retreat.

- As the participants arrive, invite them to sit at tables wherever they choose. They will sit with their friends.

- Give out small cards (or registration cards), one to each person. Have a different color card for the boys, girls and group leaders. Ask the participants to write their first and last name on the cards.

- Collect the cards yourself, being careful to keep together the cards of people who are sitting at one table.

- Decide how many groups you will need. If you need seven, for example, deal the cards into seven piles as follows: Begin with the group leaders, then distribute the cards of each group of friends. Try to balance the number of boys and girls in each group.

Playing cards   This method works well for a short session with many participants, for example, a parent-youth evening.

- Arrange three decks of cards so that each suit is in order by number, ace through king.

- Decide how many groups you will need by dividing the expected attendance by eight. This will give you seven or eight in each group; for example, if you have a total attendance of 75, you will need 10 groups. For 10 groups use only cards ace through ten in each suit.

- The way you give out the cards will assure the distribution of your participants. You will want each group to have some men, some women, some boys, some girls. Ask the men to stand and give them each a card in order—ace,2,3,4,5. . . . Then give a card to each woman, starting with whatever number is next in the pack. Next give cards to all the boys, then all the girls. Tell people not to take the same number as another member of their family. Put one card, ace through 10, in the center of each small-group circle.

- Have everyone move to the circle indicated by the number on his or her card.

- Ask someone in each group to collect the cards and bring them to you.

Count off   This is the old stand-by for grouping. Its disadvantage is that some people will "forget" their number and move to a circle of their choice rather than to the one assigned.

- Decide how many groups you will need, for example, seven.

- Ask each person to count off, from one to seven. Count off the adults first, then the girls, then the boys.

- Move to the dialogue circles one group at a time: All the "ones" follow Mr. Jones, "twos" Mrs. Smith, and so forth. Moving one group at a time makes it more difficult for a person to "forget" and move to the wrong group.

Your-choice method   Once in a while allow the young people to choose their own groups. Do this especially for shorter discussion activities of a personal nature. This works best when the groupings are just two or three people.

Retreat Rules and Regulations
(A Sample from the TYME OUT Center)

1. Alcohol and drugs   Retreatants showing evidence of having or using these substances will be sent home immediately.

2. Dormitory restriction   Girls are never allowed in the boys' dorm or boys in the girls' dorm. Likewise, no one is to leave the dormitory after lights out. Anyone breaking these rules will be sent home.

3. Safety devices   Tampering with fire extinguishers, fire alarm boxes or smoke detectors carries a $25.00 fine. (This is a city ordinance in some places. Check your own locale.)

4. Meals   Because the various groups using the center eat together family style, it is important to be on time for meals.

Each small group will be assigned to help with meal clean-up two or three times during the retreat.

Candy and snacks are available in the dining room lobby after each meal.

5. Dorms   The dorms are for sleeping only, not for lounging during the day. No food or drink is allowed in the dorms at any time.

Pillow fights are not allowed.

The dorms are kept locked during the day to protect your belongings from the other users of the building.

6. Off limits   Each group is restricted to the areas of the building assigned for its retreat.

7. Doors   Please leave the building by assigned doors only. Outside doors and corridor doors should be kept closed at all times.

8. Gym   The gym is for sensible play and fun, not for rough or destructive behavior.

Gym shoes are required.

No food or drink is allowed.

The stage area and all side rooms are off limits.

9. Smoking   Smoking is allowed only in the break rooms and outside. Please turn on the exhaust fan in the break room when smoking there.

10. Cans   Please deposit all aluminum cans in the containers marked for them.

11. *Pillows and beanbags*   The Center is provided with many pillows and beanbags for your comfort. Please do not throw the pillows or jump on the beanbags.

12. *Damage*   Please report any damage done to the building or property. Your group will be held financially responsible for the damage only if it is evident that it is the result of rowdiness or vandalism.

13. *Consideration*   We expect respect for and cooperation with the adult leaders who are giving their time to serve you on this retreat.

We expect you to be respectful of the rights and needs of your brother and sister retreatants, especially their need for a good night's sleep.

We expect respect for the other users and occupants of the building and for the neighbors, especially after 11:00 pm.

We expect respect for our building and property. Please be careful not to litter the outside grounds with candy wrappers and soda cans. Your group is expected to leave your retreat space as neat and clean as you found it.

Notes to Group Leaders
(A Sample from the TYME OUT Center)

1. Dialogue groups

Check registration cards for information regarding health, medicine and diet. Please be responsible for monitoring these items for your group.

Participate in the discussions at your table. Encourage the teen-agers to share and to listen to each other. Try to listen more than talk.

Direct your group in clean-up chores in the dining room and center.

2. Overall discipline

Try to be where the teen-agers are at all times.

Sit with the teen-agers in the dining room.

Watch especially for beanbag and pillow fights and other rowdy behavior.

3. Dorm responsibilities

Locate someone near each door.

Don't allow pillow fights or other rowdy behavior. Collect any food.

Don't allow teen-agers to be in the corridor or to leave the dorm area.

Put the lights out about 30 minutes after getting to the dorms, then request quiet.

There is a phone in the private room in the girls' dorm. Incoming emergency calls will ring there.

4. Morning

No one should get up before 7:30; everyone should be on time for breakfast at 8:30.

Turn out all the lights and lock the dorm before coming to breakfast.

On the last morning, have everyone pack up and put the pillowcases and sheets in the wash before going to breakfast.

5. Keys and change box

The leaders are given keys and a change box key. Your parish will be charged $25.00 for any key not returned.

One person should be responsible for the change box which contains $70.00. Please double check the amount with the leader before leaving. The parish will be charged for any deficit.

Please keep the dorms locked when the group is not in them. Lock the first floor corridor door when the group leaves for meals or gym.

Please do not give keys to the teen-agers.

6. Phone

Outside phones are located in the private room in the girls' dorm. These are for adult use only.

A pay phone is located in the gym lobby.

7. Tornado, Fire

If the local tornado warning sounds, bring the group to the corridor outside the dining room.

If a fire alarm sounds, lead group out by the nearest exit. Please familiarize yourself with the locations of all the fire extinguishers in the retreat area.

Sample Covers

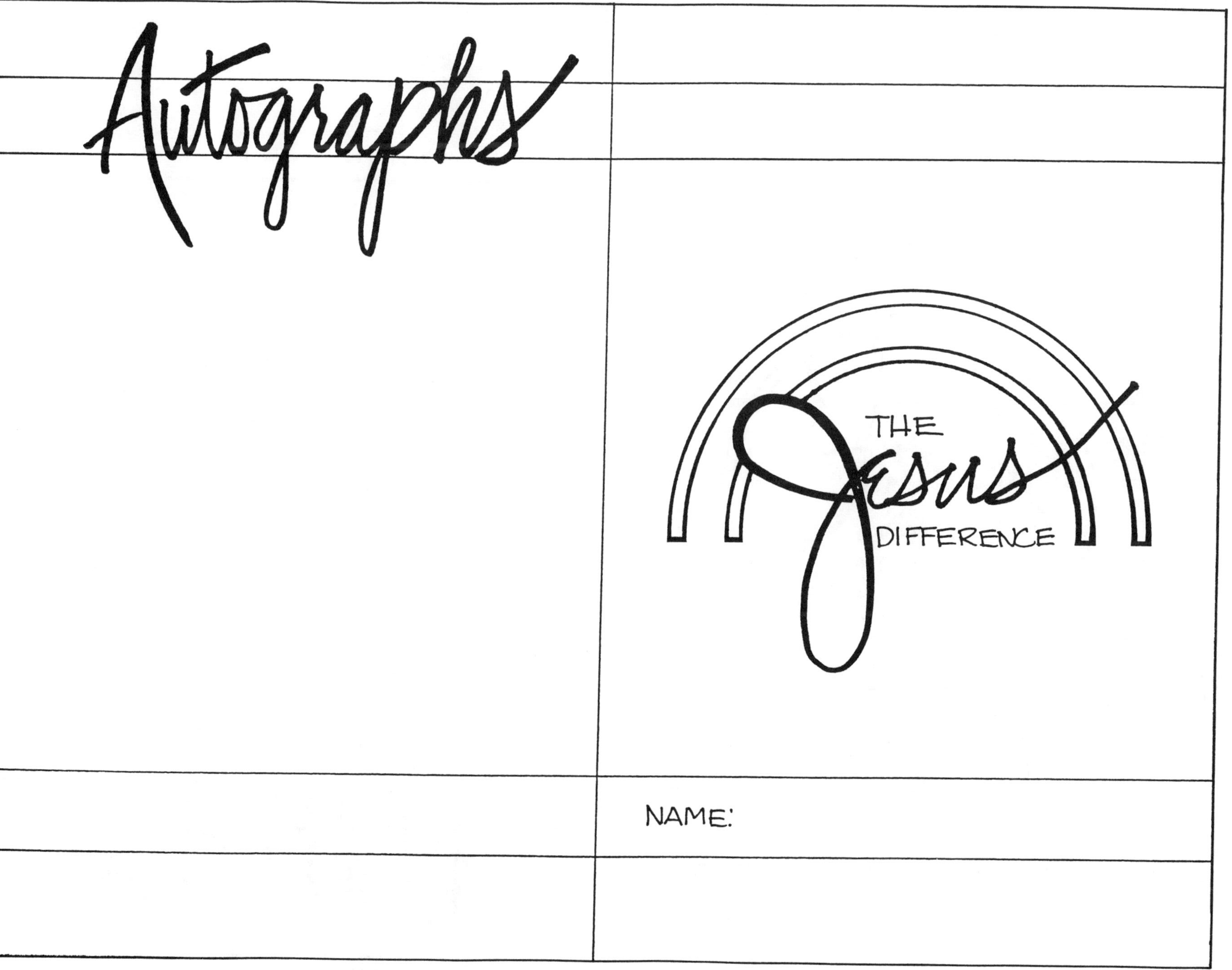

Autographs
THE
Jesus
DIFFERENCE
NAME:

Feedback

SOMETHING IMPORTANT I LEARNED ABOUT GOD DURING THIS RETREAT...

SOMETHING I LEARNED ABOUT ME...

SOMETHING I LEARNED ABOUT MY FRIENDS AND CLASSMATES...

SOMETHING I WANT TO CHANGE BECAUSE I WAS HERE...

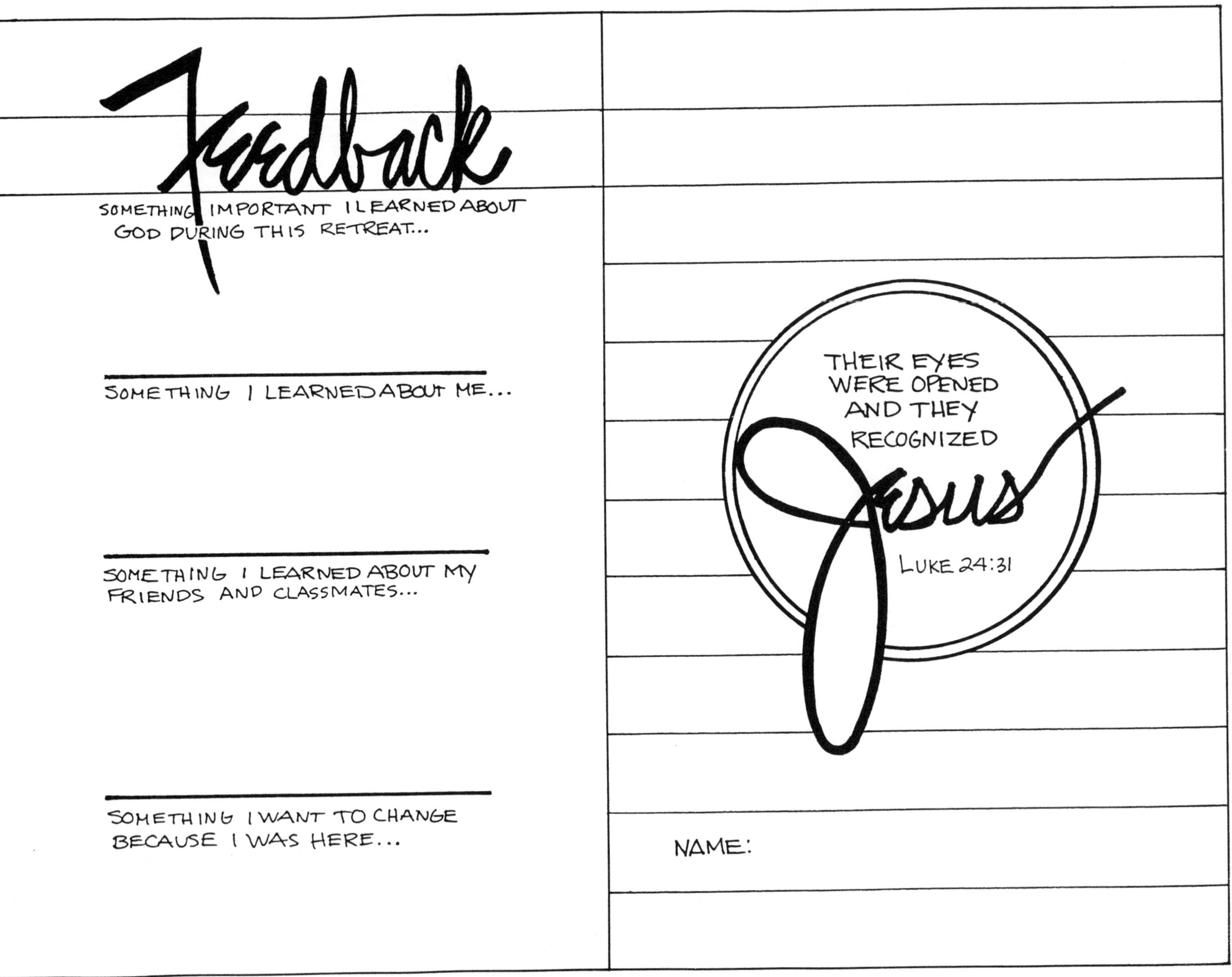

NAME:

Ask the people you shared this retreat with to sign their names in the gift boxes below.

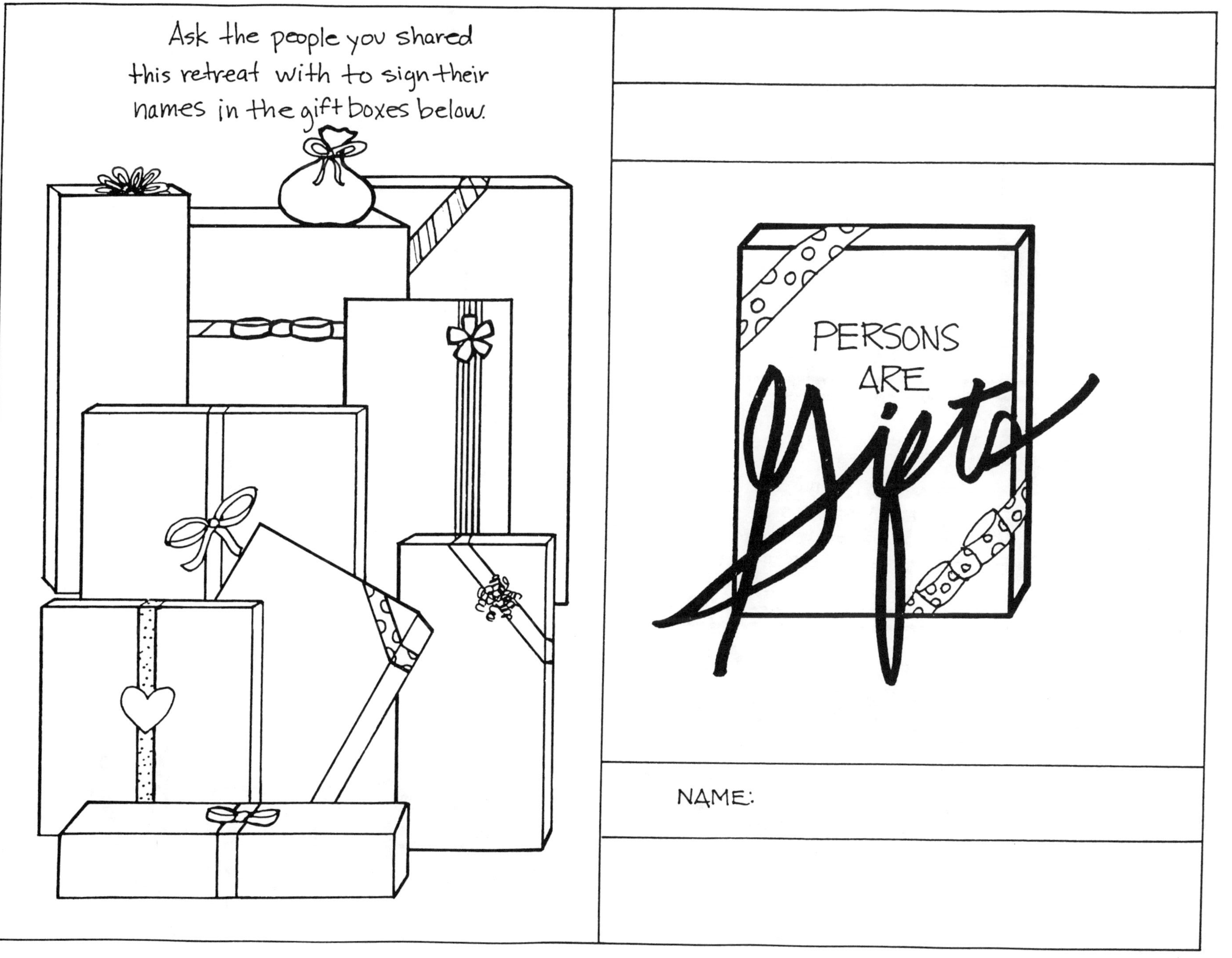

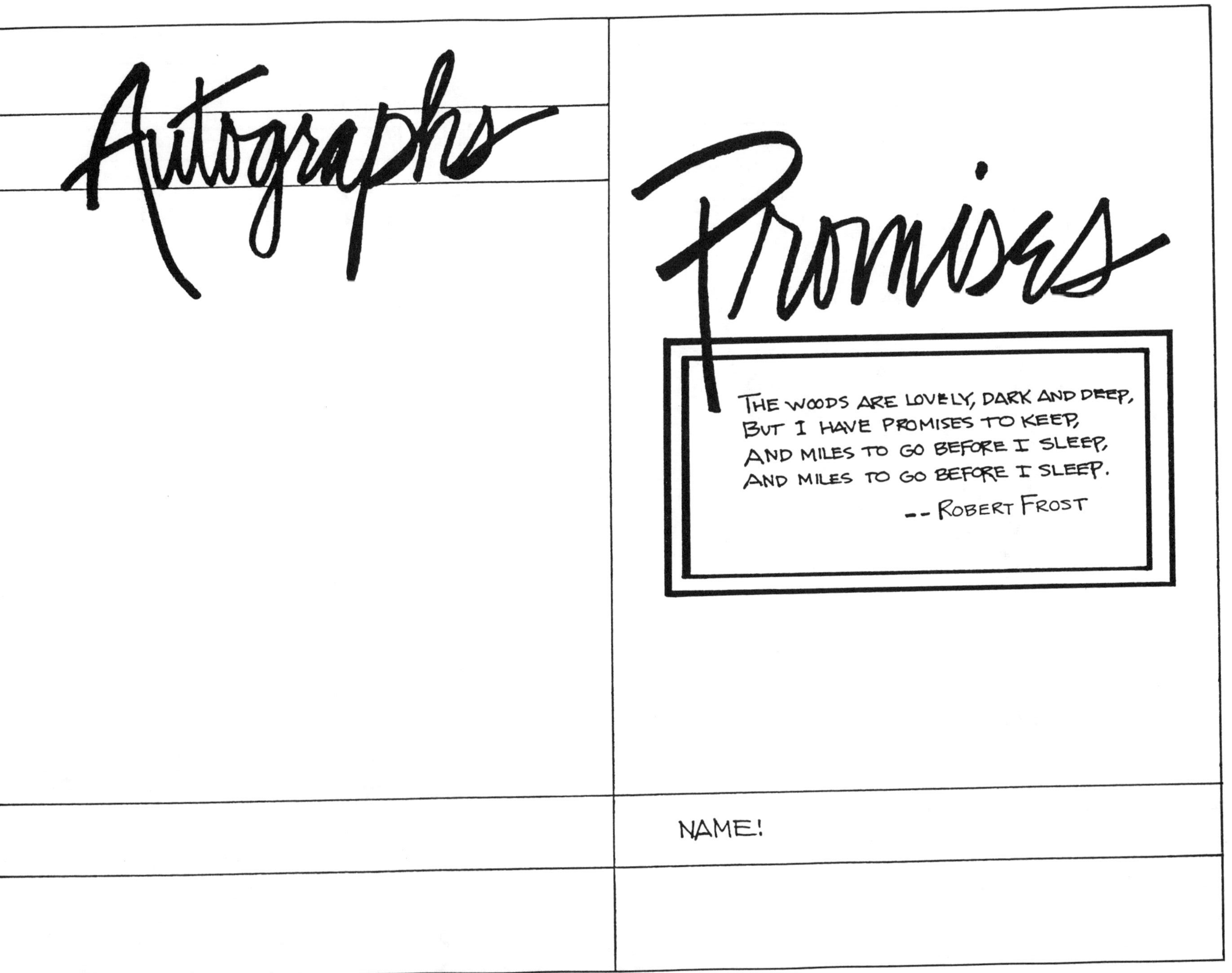

Autographs
Promises
The woods are lovely, dark and deep,
But I have promises to keep,
And miles to go before I sleep,
And miles to go before I sleep.
-- Robert Frost
NAME!

Tear-Out Section

The following pages are perforated for your convenience in copying the material you select for the participants.* Frequently material for two capsules appears side-by-side. If you choose to use only one of the capsules with your group, simply cover the other half of the tear-out sheet with blank paper before duplicating. The blank page can be used for autographs, notes, journal entries, etc.

*Permission to reprint these pages is limited to use with *The Jesus Difference* activities.

Dialogue: Why and How

The activities depend for their effectiveness on the interaction of the participants—the interaction of youth with adults, and of youth with youth. This interaction is brought about primarily through dialogue. Some of the dialogue is light, fun and humorous. Its purpose is to break down barriers and to build mutual understanding and enjoyment. It also makes serious dialogue possible. Serious dialogue, the heart of the TYME CAPSULES process, helps the participants to share with one another their dreams and hopes, their questions and doubts, their values and goals, their faith and prayer.

The dialogue process is based on several assumptions:

- that faith is already present in each person, and that dialogue helps to surface, affirm and strengthen that faith

- that each person is a source of truth and wisdom, and that the truth of each individual is meant for and needed by the entire community

- that all people, especially youth, want to open their hearts and share their deepest beliefs and doubts; all they need is listeners who care

- that talking about the deepest values in a person's life helps to clarify and strengthen them for the speaker; a person understands better what he or she has tried to articulate to another

- that the faith of the listener is also strengthened by the dialogue process; one of the most effective ways of alerting a person to the action of God in his or her life is to hear about God's action in the life of another

- that dialogue creates common meanings and values that enable those who participate in it to become a community of faith.

Dialogue of the sort described here can happen only in an atmosphere of openness and trust. To establish such an atmosphere is to a large extent the responsibility of the director. But it is also true that dialogue itself can create such an atmosphere. Young people learn to share deeply with one another and with adults by dialoguing. The director's role is to make it easy.

The dialogue activities are designed to encourage sharing. Though each activity uses a slightly different dialogue technique, some general methodological principles apply:

Pre-response   Everyone is given a chance to record his or her response in some way before being asked to respond orally. The pre-response might be written, shown with hand signals, or indicated by body positions. The responding is made easy by asking a very specific question with a definite answer, by providing sentence starters, or by giving a spread of answers to choose from. These techniques get everyone involved in thinking about the question, make it clear that there is a spread of opinion on the answer rather than one "right" response, and create the need for an individual to examine a position that is contrary to other positions presented.

Dialogue starters   Getting started with the dialogue is facilitated by designating the first speaker, often in a humorous way; for example, the person with the curliest hair, the person with the next birthday, the person wearing the most faded jeans. Each person then takes a turn around the circle. The starter designation usually creates a little burst of laughter and further relaxes the group.

Pass option   The sharing must always be done freely. If at any time a participant is asked a question he or she doesn't know how to answer, or doesn't want to answer in public, the person simply says "Pass." The pass option is, I believe, the single most effective technique in creating an atmosphere where open dialogue can happen. Given the choice of either answering honestly or passing, young people almost always choose to answer. But the pass option is always there as a safe and easy way out if they are threatened by the question in any way. It is imperative that the pass option be respected by the director and by all the participants.

Gradual deepening   The dialogue moves gradually from light, easy topics to more serious ones. The easier sharing both teaches the technique and warms the participants to one another, thus facilitating the deeper sharing.

Listening   Listening is essential to the dialogue process. Everyone in the dialogue circle shares in the listening role. It is important for all the members of the group to look at the speaker, to respond facially to what is being said, and to ask follow-up questions. The adults should be especially present to each speaker; at the same time, the adults will need to be careful not to become the focus toward which all comments or answers are directed.

The JESUS Difference

If we are true Christians, the words and actions of Jesus should make a difference in our lives. As followers of Jesus, we should try to model our lives after his, to base our attitudes and daily choices on his teaching and example.
Use the following exercise as a prayerful reflection on the Jesus difference in your everyday life.

1. Jesus often ended his teachings with the words: "Listen, if you have ears to hear."

Circle the number that indicates how good a listener you are. (1 is low, 10 is high) Put a **box** around the number that shows how well you listen when the speaker is talking about religion.

1   2   3   4   5   6   7   8   9   10

2. In one of the gospel stories, Jesus invited Peter to step out of the boat and walk toward him over the sea. Peter did, but he became frightened and called out to Jesus to save him. Jesus will probably never ask you to walk on water, but he sometimes asks you to do things that seem just as difficult.

Circle the number that indicates how likely you are to call on Jesus to help you as you walk through life's problems and temptations. (1 is very unlikely, 10 is very likely) **Box** the number that indicates how often you think he helps. (1 is never, 10 is always)

1   2   3   4   5   6   7   8   9   10

3. Jesus was often followed by a crowd of little children. When the apostles found the children annoying and tried to chase them away, Jesus stopped them and said, "Let the children come to me."

Circle the number that indicates your love and concern for little children. (1 is low, 10 is high) **Box** the number that shows how kind and loving you are to your own little brothers and sisters.

1   2   3   4   5   6   7   8   9   10

4. Jesus taught his followers to forgive those who injured them. "When someone slaps you on one cheek," he said, "turn and give him the other."

Circle the number that indicates how hard you try to forgive others. (1 is very little, 10 is very much) **Box** the number that shows how forgiving you are to your own family members.

1   2   3   4   5   6   7   8   9   10

5. One day two men were walking along behind Jesus wondering who he was and what he was like. When Jesus noticed them, they asked, "Rabbi, where do you live?" He answered, "Come and see."

Circle a number to show how much time you spend getting to know Jesus better through prayer. (1 is none, 10 is very much) **Box** a number to indicate the time you spend getting to know Jesus through reading and studying scripture.

1   2   3   4   5   6   7   8   9   10

6. One of Jesus' best-known stories is about the Good Samaritan, the unpopular person who took care of a man who had been attacked by robbers and left lying on the road.

Circle a number to show how willing you are to reach out to help people in trouble. (1 is never, 10 is always) **Box** the number that indicates your willingness to help if the person in trouble is unpopular or strange.

1   2   3   4   5   6   7   8   9   10

7. The first disciples were ordinary fishermen whom Jesus invited to follow him. Jesus is still inviting people — people like you and me — to be his followers.

Circle a number to show how much of a sense you have right now that Jesus is calling you to follow him. (1 is none, 10 is very much) **Box** a number to show how willing you are to respond to his call.

1   2   3   4   5   6   7   8   9   10

8. One gospel story tells about some people who were so eager to bring their paralyzed friend to Jesus that they made a hole in the roof to get him in.

Circle a number to show how much effort you make to help your family get closer to Jesus. (1 is none, 10 is very much) **Box** the number that indicates how much effort you make with your friends.

1   2   3   4   5   6   7   8   9   10

Jesus' Feelings

Did Jesus have feelings? If he did, how do his feelings compare to mine?

Scripture tells us that Jesus was like us in all things except sin. He must have experienced human emotions very similar to ours. Explore the New Testament to see how many of our own emotions Jesus really experienced and how he coped with them.

1. Jesus was angry. Mk 11:15ff; Mt 23:13ff

2. Jesus showed fear. Mt 26:36-38

3. Jesus was happy and could celebrate. Jn 2:1-11; Lk 10:21

4. Jesus experienced frustration. Mt 23:37ff

5. Jesus experienced personal hunger and was aware that others were hungry. Mt 4:1-2; Jn 6:1-7; Jn 4:4-8,31-34; Lk 6:1-5

6. Jesus cried. Jn 11:32-38; Lk 19:41

7. Jesus was impatient. Jn 14:8ff; Mk 10:35-45

8. Jesus felt sympathy for others. Lk 4:38ff; Mt 20:29-34; Mk 14:14; Mt 9:35ff

9. Jesus was merciful. Lk 23:39-43

10. Jesus forgave and considered forgiveness important. Lk 23:34; Lk 6:27-37; Lk 7:37-50; Mt 18:21-22; Mt 6:12-15; Mk 3:28

Luke 19

Imagine that, like Zacchaeus, Jesus comes to your house. He spends about a week with you, your family and your friends. In your mind, walk through the events and situations of a typical week. The presence of Jesus might cause you to see some things about your everyday places and people that you sometimes fail to see. Imagine what Jesus would be pleased to see happening in your family, among your friends, at your school or work. Hear what Jesus would say is displeasing to him.

Jesus says:	Jesus says:
" I am pleased with	" I am displeased with

YOUR FAMILY
because…

YOUR FRIENDS
because…

YOUR SCHOOL OR WORK PLACE
because…

YOU
because…

SCENARIOS

In each of the following scenarios:

- circle the character you most identify with or sympathize with.
- tell what you think that character should do.

PROM DATE

Tammy

Amy and Lisa

Matt

Kurt

DIAMOND EARRINGS

Mrs. Berg

Mr. Berg

Kelly

Mark

Mrs. Coleman

HOME SWEET HOME

Bob

Joe

Friends

Mom

PARTY PATTI

Patti

Val

Tracy

Kristin

REPORT CARD DAY

Mr. McMullen

Tim

Michelle

Dennis

ALL IN THE FAMILY

Gretchen

Larry

Tom

Mrs. Swanson

FOOTBALL SEASON

Coach Connely

Mike

Dave

the principal

the student body

CAUGHT

Jodi

Kim

Mr. Kreb

Reflecting & Sharing

"Then their eyes were opened and they recognized him".

First, read the following quotation. Then think about the questions on this paper and write your answers in the spaces provided. You will have about 25 minutes for this. Then gather in your small groups to discuss any answers you are willing to share.

"Two of Jesus' followers were going to a village named Emmaus, about seven miles from Jerusalem, and they were talking to each other about all the things that had happened. As they talked and discussed, Jesus himself drew near and walked along with them; they saw him, but somehow did not recognize him."

(As they traveled on together talking, Jesus said and did things that should have given them hints about who he was. He told them what the prophets had said about the resurrection, and he explained the scriptures to them, but still they did not recognize him. Eventually, they stopped their journey for supper and . . .)

"He sat down to eat with them, took the bread, and said the blessing; then he broke the bread and gave it to them. Then their eyes were opened and they recognized him" (Lk 24:13-35).

Jesus lives and is present in our world today. Maybe we don't recognize him because we don't know what to look for. Maybe we are expecting him to come only in a way we find comfortable. Or maybe we just don't take time to see that he is present in our lives. He is there for us, just as he was for the disciples on the way to Emmaus, often when we least expect him.

Questions for Reflection

1. If you had been there, walking alongside Jesus on the road to Emmaus, do you think you would have recognized him? Do you recognize him in the breaking of the bread now when you attend Mass and receive communion?

2. List five persons in whom you can see Jesus. Explain your answers.

3. List five times when, as you look back, you can recognize that Jesus was present in your life. (Both good experiences and painful or difficult situations can be occasions where we become aware of Jesus' presence.) Explain your answers.

4. On a scale of 1-10 (1 the lowest, 10 the highest), how would you rank your interest, enthusiasm and involvement in your faith? Explain.

Directions for Moderators:

The Landing of the Ishites

1. Divide the group in half, seated so they face each other. Explain:

The people on this side of the room are from the planet Ish (write the name on the board). They are called the Ishites. These folks over here are from the planet Earth. We'll call them Earthites. The Ishites land in *(name of your city)* on a morning in spring. The day seems to be very special for the Earthites. Most of them are dressed up in brand-new clothes and are headed for a tall building with a spire on top. The inside of the building is decorated with dozens of white, trumpet-like flowers. Bells are ringing and the organ is playing joyous music. There is an image in the front of the room — a man wearing only a white cloth, hanging on a cross. His hands and feet are nailed, and he has a large wound in his side. But the people seem to be very happy, not sad about it. There is some kind of ceremony taking place. The Ishites watch the entire ceremony with awe. When it is over, they corner a group of Earthites to find out what is going on. The Earthites have some difficulty answering the Ishites, but they try to explain.

2. Facilitate a discussion between the Ishites and the Earthites. Listed below are some sample Ishite questions in case your group has trouble getting started.

- Who is this man?

- How did he die?

- What did he do to deserve that?

- Why is everyone so happy if he's dead?

- How long ago did he live?

- How come everyone still remembers him?

- If he really is still here on earth, how would we recognize him if we saw him?

Recognizing Jesus in our Class

Sometimes we have difficulty finding Jesus present in those whom we are closest to and with whom we spend the majority of our time each day. Let us spend some time now reflecting on how Jesus is recognizable or not recognizable in our class.

Brainstorming:

1. Ask for a list of the positive qualities displayed in your class as a whole. Write them on the board. Do NOT talk about the behavior of individuals. Don't discuss the ideas at this time, just list as many as you can in a few minutes.

2. Ask your classmates to name the unhealthy qualities displayed in your class. List them on the board.

Open Discussion:

Spend about half an hour discussing the following questions. Give examples to verify your response. Remember to discuss how you act *as a class*. Do not respond as individuals.

1. Do you think our class is *respectful* and *considerate* toward the administration? faculty and staff? fellow students? school property? guest speakers?

2. Do you think our class is *supportive* of academics? athletics? student government? club activities?

3. Do you think our class is *reverent* during morning prayer? liturgies? prayer services? class prayer time?

4. Do you think our class is *loyal* to our school? Do we speak well of it in public by word and action?

5. Do you think our class is *united* as a group or are some people excluded and isolated because of groupings within the class?

6. Do you think that administration, faculty and staff, and other students have a good impression and feeling about our class?

Closing Prayer (10 minutes)

The closing prayer is to be prepared and conducted by the class officers.

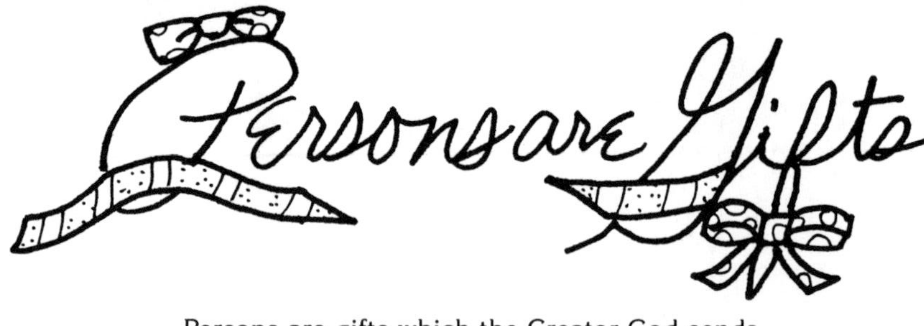
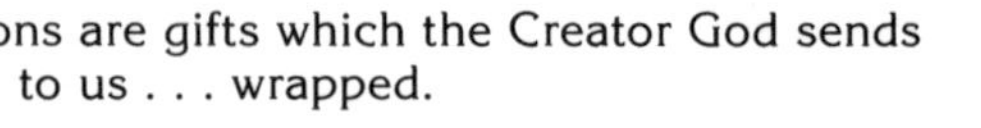

Persons are Gifts

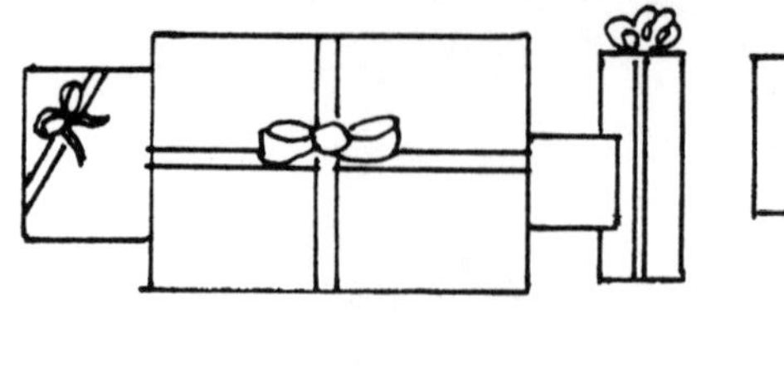
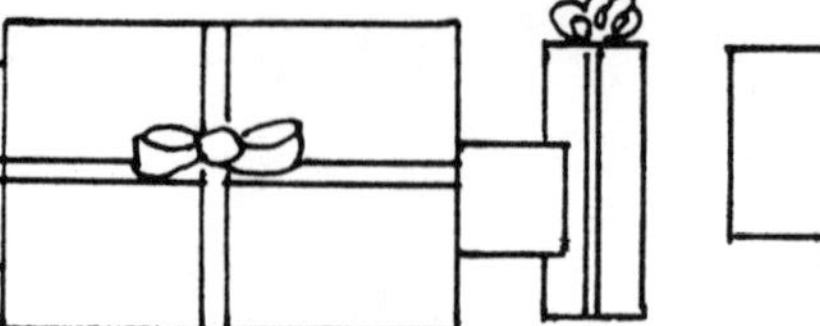

Persons are gifts which the Creator God sends
   to us . . . wrapped.

Some come wrapped very beautifully,
   some in very ordinary wrapping paper.
Some persons are very loosely wrapped,
   others very tightly.
Sometimes the gift has been mishandled in the mail.
Once in a while there is a special delivery!

But the wrapping is not the gift!
   It is so easy to make that mistake;
      it's amusing when babies do.

Some person-gifts are very easy to open up;
   others need to be helped out of their boxes.
      Is it because they are afraid?
         Do they think it might hurt to be opened?
         Maybe they have been opened up before
            and thrown away!
         Could it be that their gift is not for me?

I am a person. Therefore, I am a gift, too!
   A gift to myself, first of all.
   God my Creator gave myself to me!

Have I ever really looked inside the wrapping?
   Am I afraid to?
      Perhaps I've never accepted the gift that I am.
Could it be that there is something else
   inside the wrappings than what I think is there?
Maybe I've never seen the wonderful gift that I am.
      Could God's gift be anything but beautiful?
   I love the gifts which those who love me give to me.
   Why not the gift of me?

And I am a gift to other persons.
   Am I willing to be given to others?
      to be a person for others?
   Do others have to be content with the wrapping,
      never permitted to enjoy the gift?

Every meeting of persons is an exchange of gifts.

Love is a relationship between persons
   who see themselves as they really are:
   Gifts given by God to be given to others.

—author unknown

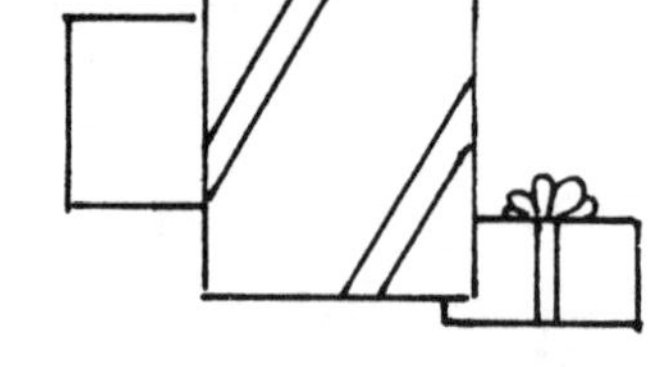

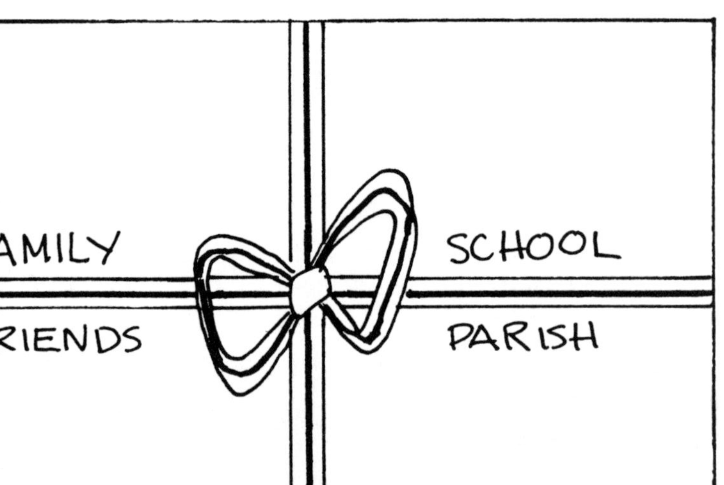

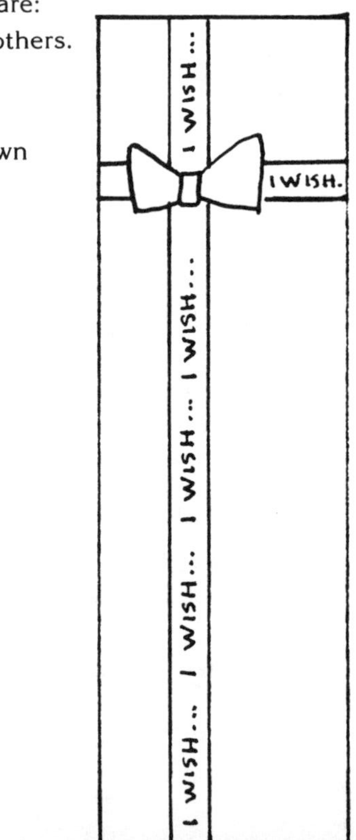

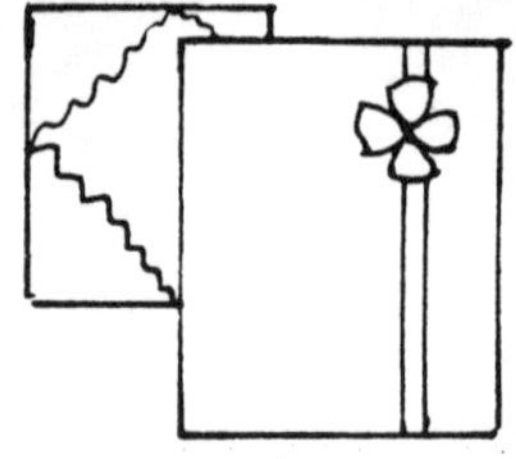

The Wrapping and the Gift

"Each one of you has received a special grace, so, like good stewards responsible for all these different graces of God, put yourselves at the service of others"

(1 Pt 4:10, JB).

THE OUTSIDE WRAPPING

Check the phrases that fit:

_____wrapped very beautifully
_____lots of bows and frills
_____brown paper and string
_____simple, classic beauty
_____wrapped in newspaper
_____mishandled in the mail
_____weather damaged
_____poked into, partly opened
_____stamped "Special Delivery"
_____stamped "Fragile"

THE INSIDE GIFT

Check the phrases that fit:

_____afraid to look
_____easily damaged
_____a special gift from God
_____packed with care
_____need help getting opened
_____willing to be shared
_____rattles around, but can't get out
_____has changed much
_____changing all the time
_____has been opened before and thrown away
_____just being discovered
_____rare treasure
_____one of a kind

1   2   3   4   5   6   7   8   9   10

Use the scale above to indicate how tightly wrapped you are. If you circle 1 it means you are a very shy and private person; a 10 indicates a very open person who is always free and open in sharing his or her thoughts and feelings.

The Wrapping Is Not the Gift

Some people come in packages that are "different" in some way—damaged, or out of shape, or strange looking, or just worn out. It takes a special kind of awareness and sensitivity to discover the real person inside such special wrappings. Sometimes we act as if the handicap is more important than the person who has it. We never give ourselves a chance to discover the beautiful person inside the different wrapping.

Check the boxes on the left to show how well you know persons with each handicap listed below.

Family Member	Close Friend	Acquaintance	
			DEAF
			BLIND
			PHYSICALLY HANDICAPPED
			MENTALLY HANDICAPPED
			SENILE
			BADLY SCARRED
			OBESE
			CHRONICALLY ILL
			"STRANGE"
			OTHER

Some reactions: fear, staring, pointing, laughter, smart remarks, over-friendliness, avoidance, shock, gentleness, concern, interest, helpfulness, pity, empathy, helplessness, derision, love, admiration

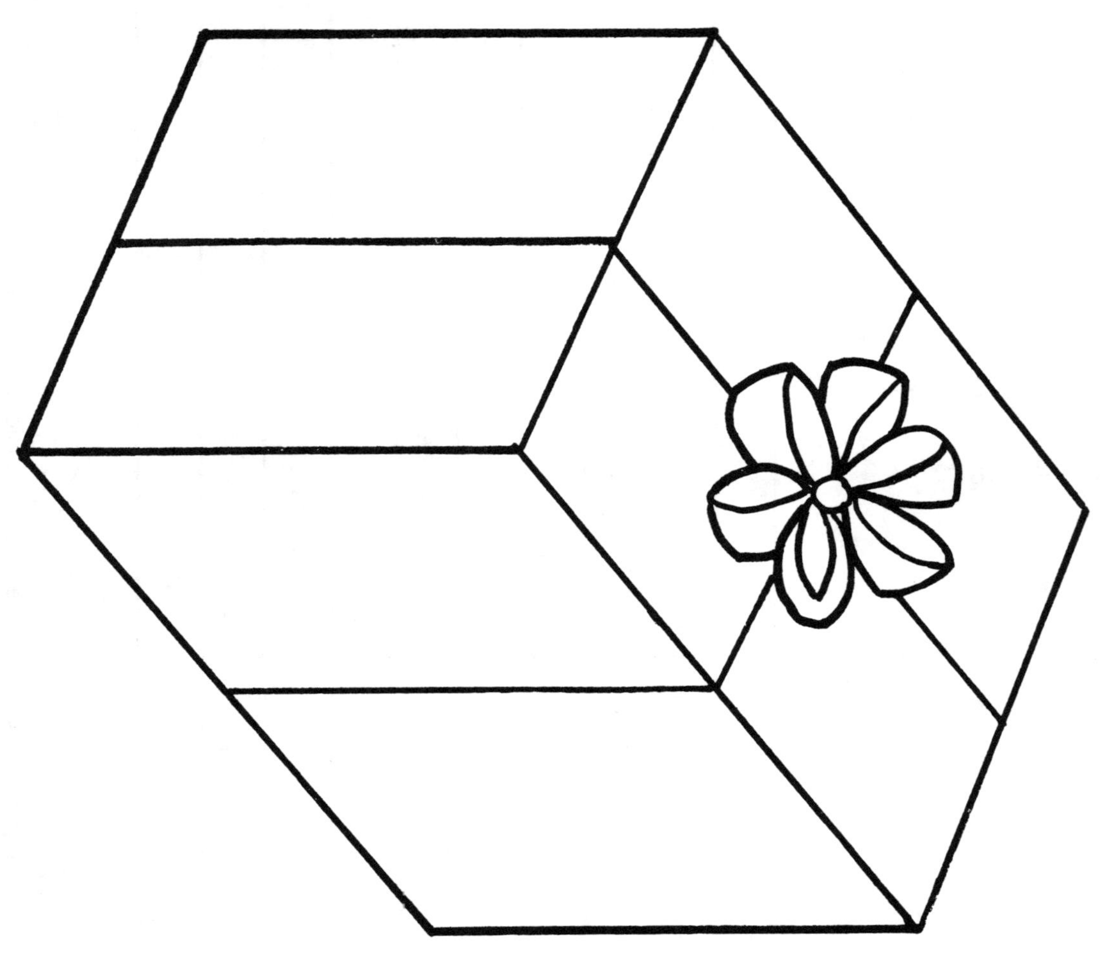

Stopping by Woods on a Snowy Evening*

Whose woods these are I think I know
His house is in the village though;
He will not see me stopping here
To watch his woods fill up with snow.

My little horse must think it queer
To stop without a farmhouse near
Between the woods and frozen lake
The darkest evening of the year.

He gives his harness bells a shake
To ask if there is some mistake.
The only other sound's the sweep
Of easy wind and downy flake.

The woods are lovely, dark and deep,
But I have promises to keep.
And miles to go before I sleep,
And miles to go before I sleep.

—Robert Frost

Faith, like so much else in life, depends on promises and commitments. God's relationship with his people is a covenant, a promise, of love: "I will be your God and you will be my people," God says to us.

In faith — I believe in God's promises. I count on him to be true to his word. I rely on his faithfulness and his love for me.

In faith — I commit myself to him and to his kingdom. I promise to give my life to him—to love him, to do his will, and to care for others the way he taught.

*From THE POETRY OF ROBERT FROST edited by Edward Connery Lathem. Copyright 1923, ©1969 by Henry Holt and Company. Copyright 1951 by Robert Frost. Reprinted by permission of Henry Holt and Company, Publishers.

Promises

A. How often do you
- promise your mom you'll clean your room? ___________
- promise to do better on your next report card? ___________
- promise to take a little brother or sister somewhere? ___________
- promise to get home early with the car? ___________
- promise to write to someone going away? ___________
- promise you won't tell a secret? ___________
- promise to pay back money you've borrowed? ___________
- promise to do the dishes—"later"? ___________
- promise God you'll do something for him? ___________
- promise to stay out of trouble? ___________
- promise yourself you'll make a change? ___________
- promise someone you'll "go steady"? ___________

Using a 1-5 scale, rate yourself as a promise keeper in each case above.

B. When you say the words "I promise," what do they mean?

______ I have given my word and I will follow through no matter what.

______ I'll try to do the thing I said I would.

______ I might do what I said if it's not too inconvenient.

______ I say the words lightly; they don't mean anything.

______ Other: ___________________________________

C. *Commitments.* A commitment is a deep inner promise made either to yourself or to others. List some of your personal commitments in the boxes below.

person or relationship	team or organization	job or task
goal	ideal or value	cause

GOD'S Promises to me:

_____ The LORD said: "Call to me and I will answer you; I will tell you wonderful and marvelous things that you know nothing about" (Jeremiah 33:3).

_____ And so I am sure that God who began this good work in you will carry it on until it is finished on the Day of Christ Jesus (Philippians 1:6).

_____ God is able to give you more than you need, so that you will always have all you need for yourself and more than enough for every good cause (2 Corinthians 9:8).

_____ I have the strength to face all conditions by the power that Christ gives me (Philippians 4:13).

_____ We know that in all things God works for good with those who love him (Romans 8:28).

_____ But those who trust in the LORD for help
will find their strength renewed.
They will rise on wings like eagles;
they will run and not get weary;
they will walk and not grow weak (Isaiah 40:31).

_____ "Ask and you will receive; seek and you will find; knock, and the door will be opened to you. For everyone who asks will receive, and anyone who seeks will find, and the door will be opened to him who knocks" (Matthew 7:7).

_____ Every test that you have experienced is the kind that normally comes to people. But God keeps his promise, and he will not allow you to be tested beyond your power to remain firm; at the time you are put to the test, he will give you the strength to endure it, and so provide you with a way out (1 Corinthians 10:13).

_____ "Listen! I stand at the door and knock; if anyone hears my voice and opens the door, I will come into his house and eat with him, and he will eat with me" (Revelations 3:20).

_____ Who, then, can separate us from the love of Christ? Can trouble do it, or hardship or persecution or hunger or poverty or danger or death? . . . No, in all these things we have complete victory through him who loved us! For I am certain that nothing can separate us from his love: neither death nor life, neither angels nor other heavenly rulers or powers, neither the present nor the future, neither the world above nor the world below—there is nothing in all creation that will ever be able to separate us from the love of God which is ours through Christ Jesus our Lord (Romans 8:35-39).

_____ I will always guide you and satisfy you with good things. I will keep you strong and well. You will be like a garden that has plenty of water, like a spring of water that never goes dry (Isaiah 58:11).

_____ "I will ask the Father, and he will give you another Helper, who will stay with you forever. He is the Spirit who reveals the truth about God" (John 14:16).

_____ "Whoever loves me will obey my teaching. My Father will love him, and my Father and I will come to him and live with him" (John 14:23).

_____ "Go, then, to all peoples everywhere and make them my disciples: . . . teach them to obey everything I have commanded you. And I will be with you always, to the end of the age" (Matthew 28:19-20).

my promise to GOD:

Directions for Guides:

Trust Walk

- Select a "blind" person, one of the opposite sex if possible

- Keep perfect silence

- Lead your person through many different experiences:

  touch things of various textures

  go up and down stairs

  listen to noises

  smell flowers, leaves

  bounce a ball; play simple catch; jump rope

  (add other appropriate experiences)

- Stay within sight of the retreat director

- Be gentle; be careful; be trustworthy

- Try not to give yourself away

- Bring the person back to the group and remove the blindfold

- Show the person the directions and ask him or her to take one of the remaining blindfolded people for a walk

- Select another person to take for a walk

TRUST WALK REFLECTION SHEET

1. Describe the feelings you had as you were led on the trust walk.

2. What was your most significant experience during the trust walk?

3. What did you discover about yourself during this walk?

4. Describe your partner, basing your impressions totally on what you experienced during the trust walk.

5. What kind of guide were *you*—patient, mean, irresponsible, trustworthy, caring, gentle, teasing?

6. Did this trust walk bring any experience from your past to mind? Describe briefly.

A Hymn of Praise

Sing to the LORD, all the world!
Worship the LORD with joy;
    Come before him with happy songs!

Acknowledge that the LORD is God.
    He made us and we belong to him;
    we are his people, we are his flock.

Enter the Temple gates with thanksgiving;
    go into its courts with praise.
    Give thanks to him and praise him.

The LORD is good;
    his love is eternal
    and his faithfulness lasts forever (Ps 100).

Friendship Frame

Value Indicators

1. OBEYING RULES _____ _____ _____
2. JOINING A CLUB _____ _____ _____
3. GOING TO CLASS DRUNK OR HIGH _____ _____ _____
4. READING THE BIBLE _____ _____ _____
5. WEARING DESIGNER JEANS _____ _____ _____
6. HELPING TEACHERS _____ _____ _____
7. SELLING DRUGS TO CHILDREN _____ _____ _____
8. SEX BEFORE MARRIAGE _____ _____ _____
9. SHOPLIFTING _____ _____ _____
10. CUTTING DOWN TEACHERS _____ _____ _____
11. DRIVING DRUNK OR STONED _____ _____ _____
12. TALKING ABOUT GOD _____ _____ _____
13. COPYING HOMEWORK _____ _____ _____
14. BAD-MOUTHING PARENTS _____ _____ _____
15. GETTING HOME ON TIME _____ _____ _____
16. VANDALISM _____ _____ _____
17. BRAGGING ABOUT SEXUAL CONQUESTS _____ _____ _____
17. CHEATING ON TESTS _____ _____ _____
19. GOING OUT FOR SPORTS _____ _____ _____
20. GETTING GOOD GRADES _____ _____ _____
21. SMOKING CIGARETTES _____ _____ _____

5 — PRAISED! (IN)
4 — ENCOURAGED
3 — ACCEPTED
2 — TOLERATED
1 — REJECTED (OUT)

22. PEPSI PARTIES _____ _____ _____
23. LYING TO PARENTS _____ _____ _____
24. "BS"ING TEACHERS _____ _____ _____
25. DRESSING UP FOR SCHOOL _____ _____ _____
26. GOING TO CHURCH _____ _____ _____
27. ABORTION _____ _____ _____
28. UNCHAPERONED PARTIES _____ _____ _____
29. SUPPORTING EQUAL RIGHTS _____ _____ _____
30. PUTTING DOWN UNPOPULAR KIDS _____ _____ _____
31. FIGHTING _____ _____ _____
32. REGISTERING FOR THE DRAFT _____ _____ _____
33. USING TABLE MANNERS _____ _____ _____
34. VULGAR LANGUAGE _____ _____ _____
35. SMOKING POT _____ _____ _____
36. REPORTING TROUBLE (NARKING) _____ _____ _____
37. CARRYING WEAPONS _____ _____ _____
38. GOING ON A RETREAT (VOLUNTARILY) _____ _____ _____
39. SINGING IN CHURCH _____ _____ _____
40. ATTENDING X-RATED MOVIES _____ _____ _____
41. DRIVING ABOVE THE SPEED LIMIT, DRAGGING _____ _____ _____
42. BEING POLITE TO ADULTS _____ _____ _____
43. SUPPORTING A NUCLEAR FREEZE _____ _____ _____
44. EATING HEALTH FOOD _____ _____ _____

Footprints in the Sand

One night I had a dream. I dreamed I was walking along the beach with the Lord. Across the sky flashed scenes from my life. For each scene, I noticed two sets of footprints in the sand; one belonging to me, and the other to the Lord.

When the last scene of my life flashed before me, I looked back at the footprints in the sand. I noticed that many times along the path of my life there was only one set of footprints. I also noticed that it happened at the very lowest and saddest times in my life.

This really bothered me and I questioned the Lord about it. "Lord, you said that once I decided to follow you, you'd walk with me all the way. But I have noticed that during the most troublesome times in my life, there is only one set of footprints. I don't understand why when I needed you most you would leave me."

The Lord replied, "My precious, precious child, I love you and I would never leave you. During your times of trial and suffering, when you see only one set of footprints, it was then that I carried you."

—author unknown

(A poster containing this poem is distributed by Argus Communications, Allen, Texas, 1982.)

Here I Am, Lord

Then I heard the Lord say,
"Whom shall I send? Who will be our messenger?"

I answered,
"I will go! Send me!"

I will hold your people in my heart

Scripture Prayer

Matthew 5:13-16	Matthew 9:9-12
Mark 9:33-41	Mark 11:22-25
Luke 6:43-45	Luke 12:22-31
John 10:11-16	John 15:1-4
1 Corinthians 9:23-27	Ephesians 3:14-21

I have called you by name - you are mine. When you pass through deep waters, I will be with you; your troubles will not overwhelm you ... You are precious to me ... I love you ... I love you and give you honor. "Do not Be afraid - I will save you."

**Do not Be afraid —
I am with you!"**

(Is 43:1-5).

Dear God, life really confuses me sometimes... I wish you would help me with... you say that you love me, but... I have a problem with... you've given me much to be grateful for... What would really make me happy... I promise... please forgive me for...

Preparation for the Sacrament of Reconciliation

1. Quiet your mind and heart and ask the Holy Spirit to be with you. Pray that God will help you to see your inner self as he sees you—with all your strengths and all your faults. Ask him to help you to be absolutely honest with yourself and with the priest.

2. Spend some time examining your conscience. Consider your actions and attitudes in each area of your life. Ask yourself, "Is this area of my life pleasing to God or not?"

Faith
- daily prayer
- attendance and participation at Mass
- use of God's name
- respect for sacred persons, places, things
- religious education

Family
- respectful, loving relationship with parents
- concern for brothers and sisters
- responsibility and helpfulness at home
- truthfulness
- forgiveness

School and Work
- respect for teachers and peers
- serious study habits
- honesty on tests and assignments
- response to criticism and correction
- punctuality and responsibility
- friendliness, kindness

Fun
- use of drugs and alcohol
- respect for property — vandalism, stealing
- responsible driving habits
- respect for authority
- choice of entertainment—movies, TV, books
- respectful language
- peer pressure

Sexuality and Relationships
- truthfulness and honesty
- respect and responsibility
- sexual control, chastity

3. Approach the priest for confession. Once you enter the confession room, you will have a choice of either kneeling behind the screen or sitting face-to-face with the priest. He will welcome you in the name of Jesus and the church.

4. Make the sign of the cross with the priest. He will say: "May God who has enlightened every heart help you to know your sins and to trust in his mercy."

You reply: **"Amen."**

5. Confess your sins to the priest. Simply and directly talk to him about the areas of sinfulness in your life that need God's healing touch.

6. The priest will talk to you about your life, encourage you to be more faithful to God in the future, and help you decide what to do to make up for your sins—your penance.

7. The priest will ask you to make an act of contrition. You can pray in your own words, telling God that you are sorry for your sins and that you want to love him better, or you can recite this prayer:

"O my God, I am sorry for my sins. In choosing to sin, and failing to do good, I have sinned against you and your people. I firmly intend, with the help of your Son, to make up for my sins and to love you as I should. Amen."

8. The priest will extend his hands over your head and pray the church's official prayer of absolution: "God, the Father of mercies, through the death and resurrection of his Son has reconciled the world to himself and sent the Holy Spirit among us for the forgiveness of sins; through the ministry of the Church may God give you pardon and peace, and I absolve you from your sins in the name of the Father, and of the Son, and of the Holy Spirit."

You respond: **"Amen."**

9. The priest will wish you peace. Be sure to thank him as you leave.

10. Return to your place and spend some time quietly thanking God for his loving forgiveness. Don't forget to do your penance.

Psalm 139

Lord, you have examined me and you know me.
You know everything I do;
    from far away you understand all my thoughts.
You see me, whether I am working or resting;
    you know all my actions.
Even before I speak,
    you already know what I will say.
You are all around me on every side;
    you protect me with your power.
Your knowledge of me is too deep;
    it is beyond my understanding.

Where could I go to escape from you?
    Where could I get away from your presence?
If I went up to heaven, you would be there;
    if I lay down in the world of the dead, you would be there.
If I flew away beyond the east
    or lived in the farthest place in the west,
you would be there to lead me,
    you would be there to help me.
I could ask the darkness to hide me
    or the light around me to turn into night,
but even darkness is not dark for you,
    and the night is as bright as the day.
    Darkness and light are the same to you.

You created every part of me;
    you put me together in my mother's womb.
I praise you because you are to be feared;
    all you do is strange and wonderful.
    I know it with all my heart.
When my bones were being formed,
    carefully put together in my mother's womb,
when I was growing there in secret,
    you knew that I was there—
    you saw me before I was born.
The days allotted to me
    had all been recorded in your book,
    before any of them ever began.
O God, how difficult I find your thoughts,
    how many of them there are!
If I counted them, they would be more than the grains of sand.
    When I awake, I am still with you. . . .

Examine me, O God, and know my mind;
    test me, and discover my thoughts.
Find out if there is any evil in me
    and guide me in the everlasting way.

RESPONSE:

THE THOUGHT OF GOD BEING THIS CLOSE

☐ SCARES ME
☐ AWES ME
☐ WORRIES ME
☐ EMBARRASSES ME
☐ OVERWHELMS ME WITH JOY
☐ MYSTIFIES ME
☐ SHOCKS ME
☐ CONSOLES ME
☐ BORES ME
☐ AMAZES ME
☐ MAKES LITTLE DIFFERENCE TO ME

WHEN GOD EXAMINES MY HEART, HE FINDS THAT I AM

☐ CONFUSED
☐ REALLY TRYING TO PLEASE HIM
☐ TRYING TO HIDE FROM HIM
☐ TRYING TO HIDE FROM MYSELF
☐ EAGER TO KNOW HIS WILL
☐ PRETENDING
☐ AFRAID
☐ REBELLIOUS
☐ EMPTY
☐ TOO BUSY WITH OTHER CONCERNS

In him we Live and Move and have our being. — Acts 17:28

Mass Preparation

1. Setting

- Determine where the Mass will be celebrated and prepare the space: altar, seating, lighting, decorations.
- Set the altar table: table cloth, candles, flowers.
- Prepare the bread and wine, plate and cup, liturgical books.
- Decide how the gifts will be presented.
- Prepare the vestments (check with the celebrant in advance).
- Appoint eucharistic ministers.

2. Music

- Select songs and acclamations that fit the theme of the retreat.
- Form a small group to lead the singing.
- Assign someone to introduce each song.
- Choose recorded meditation music to be played during the reception of communion.
- Give out and collect the song books.

3. Readings

- Select readings that fit the theme of the retreat.
- Determine how you want to present the readings. — Plan introductions for each reading, short explanations telling why the reading was chosen and what to listen for.
- Choose readers and practice with them.

4. Creed

- Prepare an original creed stating in your own words the faith of your group. Be sure to include what you believe about God the Father, about his Son Jesus and about the Holy Spirit.
- Choose a person or group to present the creed.

5. Prayer of the Faithful

- Prepare five or six petitions that flow from the content of the retreat. Remember the needs of the world, of the church, of the poor and oppressed, of your own parish and family.
- Choose a response for the petitions; for example, Lord, hear our prayer; Hear us, O God; Stay with us, Lord Jesus.
- Determine how you will present the petitions: one reader for all, different readers for each, or some other way.

6. Communion Meditation

Prepare and present a reflection experience to be used after communion. Some possibilities:

- a reflective reading
- a musical number, recorded or live
- a litany of thanksgiving
- a slide show
- a simple liturgical dance
- a faith-sharing activity such as passing a candle or witness statements.

Cozy Corner Directions

1. Put the cards face down in the center of the group. Explain that the cards with stars are "riskier" questions, that is, they ask about deeper values.

2. *Person A* picks a card, reads it silently, and decides to whom to direct the question. *A* then reads the question directly to *Person B*, for example, "John, what do you believe happens to the human person after death?" If there are two questions on a card, wait for the answer to the first before reading the second.

3. *Person B* answers the question. *Person A* then responds, by agreeing or disagreeing, by giving his or her own answer, by asking a follow-up question, and so forth.

4. *Person A* then asks if anyone else in the group wants to comment. *Person A* might also ask to hear *everyone*'s answer to the question.

5. *Person B* selects a new question and proceeds as above.

What is your attitude
toward violence?

*

If you should parent a child before
marriage, how much would you be
willing to give up for the child?

**

Do you think people are really
good at heart? Are you?

Tell about a person (not a relative)
that you can truly say is your
brother or sister?

What rights does a baby have?
What rights does a fetus have?

*

What do you believe happens to
the human person after death?

*

How would you deal with a good
friend you knew was getting deeply
involved in drugs?

**

How would you deal with a friend
who is getting seriously
drunk several times a week?

**

Tell about an event that happened in
your family or in your own experience
that you would call a miracle.

*

What are some of the things you
can and should do to make your
home a happier place?

How do you react when you see a child
being bullied? How do you react when the
bully's victim is an unpopular teen-ager?

*

What would you do if you found
a wallet containing $500?

What would be your response to an invitation to spend your life as a priest, a sister, or a brother?

*

What do you remember as the greatest day of your life?

Explain to the group how you feel when you love someone.

**

Name one adult at school or at work whom you admire. Tell why.

On what basis do you select your same-sex friends? your opposite-sex friends?

Select a word or phrase that best describes your life at this time.

Describe a true friend. How many friends do you have that fit that description?

What person has most influenced your life? Try to tell how the person has affected you.

*

What are your personal convictions about using marijuana and other drugs?

*

What change would you make in the church if you were pope?

Name a person your age that you admire. Tell why.

What is your greatest fear?

*

Name something that usually angers
you and tell why. How do you react
when you become angry?

What is the greatest value
that guides your life?

When was the last time you
really prayed about something?
Was your prayer answered?

What do you think people like in you
the most? What about you do you
think people might find annoying?

**

Select a word that you feel describes
people your age. Explain.

Share something that you like
about your family. Share something
that bugs you about them.

In school you have seen certain
people all year and have seldom or
never spoken to them. Explain why not.

What was your best year in school?
your worst year?

What is the most difficult thing
you have ever done?

If you had to find a new name for
God (a non-religious name),
what word would you use?

**

When was the last time
you cried and why?

Tell about a turning point in
your life.

*

**

One-on-One Dialogue — Adult Leaders

1. Begin the dialogue by greeting the young person by name. Encourage a bit of small talk to help her or him become comfortable.

2. Ask any of the questions below. Feel free to ask others based on the needs and interests of the person you are talking to.

Retreat
- How is the retreat going for you?
- How much of yourself are you putting into it?
- What did you expect it to be like?
- Which activities have you found most helpful? difficult? boring? challenging?
- Would you want to go on a retreat again?

Confirmation Preparation (if applicable)
- What have you liked about your confirmation program? disliked?
- How have you cooperated?
- What have you been doing for service projects?
- How ready do you feel you are to be confirmed?
- Would you delay confirmation if you decided you are not ready?

Prayer
- Do you pray every day? when? where? how?
- Do you ever read the Bible on your own? Would you consider trying to do that regularly?
- What is your attitude toward Sunday Mass? Are you improving? Are you working at improving?

Family
- What is your attitude at home?
- How do you feel about your relationship with your mother? father? brothers and sisters?
- What would your parents like to see you improve in—besides grades?
- What could you do to make your family a happier place?

Confession (if it is being offered)
- How do you feel about going to confession today?
- Do you have any questions about what to do or say? (If the person seems hesitant, encourage him or her to use this chance to receive the sacrament of reconciliation.)

Vocation
- Do you know what you want to be when you "grow up"?
- Have you ever considered your vocation? Do you think you might be called to marriage? to the single life? to religious life? Have you thought about being a lay minister?

3. Ask if there is anything else the young person would like to talk about.

4. Close with a short prayer and/or one of the following blessings:

May the Lord bless you and keep you.
May his face shine upon you and be gracious to you.
May he look upon you with kindness and give you his peace.

or

May the blessing of God rest upon you.
May his peace abide with you.
May his presence illuminate your heart, now and forevermore.

or

__________ *(Name)* __________**, I commend you to the Holy Spirit, through the most powerful intercession of the Blessed Virgin Mary, and I entrust you forever to her blessed hands.**

One-on-One Dialogue — Youth Leaders

1. Greet your dialogue partner by name and make sure he or she is comfortable.

2. Ask some of the following questions, or any other questions you think would fit the person and the situation.

Retreat
- Have you ever been on a retreat before?
- How does this retreat compare to the other(s)? How is it different from what you may have expected?
- What did you like best about what we've done so far? least?
- Would you consider coming back as a youth leader?

School
- How is school going this year?
- Do you have any favorite classes? any that you hate?
- What's the general attitude toward the teachers and administration in your school?
- What's the drug-alcohol problem like at your school? Are you involved in any peer programs to try to help kids who have these problems?
- Does your school have a branch of SADD (Students Against Drunk Driving)? How effective is it?

Family
- Do you have older brothers or sisters? younger?
- How do you get along with everyone at home?

- Are your parents strict?
- What things do you like to do with your family?

Friends and Fun
- Who are your best friends right now? Tell me about them.
- Are cliques a problem in your school?
- How does your friendship group fit into the pecking order?
- What do you usually do for fun?
- Are you into sports? music? plays? parties?

Parish
- Does your parish have an active youth group?
- What does it do?
- Are *you* involved in anything at church?
- Does your parish offer Masses that are geared to youth?

Work
- Do you have a job? How many hours?
- Do you like your job? What is your boss like? Is it hard to get off for things like this retreat?
- Is this the kind of work you would like to do for a living?
- Do you find it hard to keep up with all your commitments—work, school, church, friends, family?

3. Close the dialogue by reciting together St. Francis' prayer for peace. Give the person the prayer as a memento.

prayer for peace

Lord, make me an instrument of your peace:
where there is hatred, let me sow love;
where there is injury, pardon;
where there is doubt, faith;
where there is despair, hope;
where there is darkness, light;
and where there is sadness, joy.

O Divine Master,
grant that I may not so much seek
to be consoled as to console;
to be understood as to understand;
to be loved as to love;
for it is in giving that we receive;
it is in pardoning that we are pardoned;
and it is in dying that we
are born to eternal life.

+ attributed to St. Francis

Jesus Interview

What do you think is the biggest problem in the world? Is there something you think I should do about it? What are *you* doing to solve it?

Do you think your religion classes have helped or hindered your love for me?

How well do you know my Father? Have my followers done a good job of telling you about him?

What do you think about my church? Do you think it's going the way I planned? How would you suggest it be improved?

What would you like me to do for your family? for you? for your friends?

Are you afraid to die? What do you think I meant when I said, "Those who believe in me will never die"?

Do you know anyone who truly lives the way I expect people to live? Tell me about him or her. Would you like to live that way? What seems to be the biggest obstacle for you?

Are you usually happy? What do you need to make you happier than you are? Is there anything that could make you perfectly happy? Can I help?

May I come to your house for dinner? How will you introduce me? Do you think the dinner table will be different because I am there?

Would you like to be my friend? I seem to have trouble making friends in your school. What do you think my problem is?

May I spend the whole day with you tomorrow? How do you think the day will go with me along? How would you explain me to your friends?

My church needs dynamic, prayerful leaders. But I seem to be having trouble recruiting people your age these days. What do you think I should do to encourage you and your peers to work for me?

God Questions

_____ What kind of mental image do you use for God?

_____ Do you think of God in human form?

_____ Do you have separate images for Jesus and for God the Father?

_____ Is your God male or female or androgynous?

_____ What role does God play in human life?

_____ When we pray for people who are sick, does God make them better?

_____ Does God give farmers rain when they pray for it?

_____ When two teams are playing a game and both teams are praying to win, does God choose sides?

_____ Are most people basically good or basically evil?

_____ Where do you look for moral guidance in your life?

_____ Do you still follow your parents' moral teachings? Should you?

_____ What is the best way to train children to be good moral persons?

_____ What do you believe about life after death?

_____ How do you understand heaven and hell?

_____ Do you plan on going to heaven someday?

_____ Do you know anyone who you are sure is now in heaven?

_____ How do you pray?

_____ When and where do you pray?

_____ Is it better to pray formula prayers or to use your own words?

_____ Do you have a sense of God's presence when you pray?

_____ Do you think God really listens and cares?

DICE DICE **1**	DOCTOR DOCTOR **6**	LE VEL **11**	T O W N (vertical) **16**
ECNALG **2**	R|E|A|D|I|N|G **7**	R O A D / ROAD (crossword) **12**	SAND (boxed) **17**
<u>WEAR</u> LONG **3**	K C E H C (vertical) **8**	0-144 **13**	GROUND FEET FEET FEET FEET FEET FEET **18**
C with SE / 8DO inside circle **4**	<u>MIND</u> MATTER **9**	KNEE LIGHT **14**	DATE DATE **19**
L K YOU O O **5**	T O U C H (vertical) **10**	CHAIR **15**	<u>STAND</u> I **20**

CYCLE CYCLE CYCLE **21**	† † **26**	house PRAIRIE **31**	Horoomtel Moroomtel INN **36**
OFF **22**	E L U C L L I C **27**	RIGHT = RIGHT **32**	SEARCH AND **37**
HE'S / HIMSELF **23**	**T.V.** **28**	<u>SLEEPING</u> JOB **33**	25¢ REFUND **38**
SIDE / SIDE **24**	SOUP **29**	E G S G S E G G G E G S S G G E **34**	m ce m ce m ce **39**
<u>MAN</u> BOARD **25**	GUN, Jr. **30**	0 ――――― Ph.D M.D. M.A. L L. D. **35**	1. D 5. U 2. R 6. L 3. A 7. A 4. C **40**